'If you are what you own, then you sl[...] It will make you knowledgeable, cha[...] once again takes an incredibly comple[...] [...] and demystifies it in a way that is still a great pleasure to read.'

Tracey Follows

Forbes Top 50 female futurist,
Visiting Professor in Digital Futures and
Identity at Staffordshire University,
author of *The Future of You*

'*It's Mine* directs our gaze toward the power of epoch-defining change while marking the course with the practical application of digital ownership. Future historians may well look back on *It's Mine* and wonder at such a heuristic prescience gilded with clarity, style, and grace.'

Josh Rosenthal

Historian, podcaster, public intellectual,
educator, serial entrepreneur

'Sidley explains clearly and persuasively how our rights and identities are being changed and challenged by technologies of our own making, and how, in turn, these changes could unravel and rewrite so many of the human constructs and necessary fictions – including money, citizenship, and property rights – we've held to be self-evident.'

Bronwyn Williams

Futurist, economist partner at Flux Trends
and Metanomic and author of
The Future Starts Now

'I found Sidley's different perspective on the crypto scene both thought-provoking and useful.'

David Birch

Senior Research Fellow, Kings College, London,
author of *The Currency Cold War* and
Before Babylon, Beyond Bitcoin

IT'S MINE

IT'S MINE

How the Crypto Industry
Is Redefining Ownership

Steven Boykey Sidley

HERO, AN IMPRINT OF LEGEND TIMES GROUP LTD
51 Gower Street
London WC1E 6HJ
United Kingdom
www.hero-press.com

First published by Hero in 2023

© Steven Boykey Sidley, 2023

The right of the author to be identified as the author of this work has
been asserted in accordance with the Copyright, Designs and Patents
Act 1988. British Library Cataloguing in Publication Data available.

Printed in Great Britain

ISBN: 978-1-91564-351-3

It's Mine

Introduction

THE GROUND ON WHICH
THE CREATURES WALK

Like most people going about their business in the early 2020s, concerned and dispirited by the pandemic and political polarization and the disturbing mutations of power wrought by social media, the emergence of a squealing baby called NFTs was a small bewilderment.

I was already deep into blockchain technology and its combustive innovations, having just finished a book with co-writer Simon Dingle called *Beyond Bitcoin: Decentralised Finance and the End of Banks*. But this new blockchain-borne species was a mote in the corner of my eye, lightly disturbing my view of the future. What were they doing? Who were these people paying seemingly irrational amounts for sometimes questionable collections of pixels on a screen?

It didn't stop there. There was a continuing confusion of new amorphous shapes forming around crypto innovations – tantalizing hints of a new sort of Internet, opportunities to own a piece of immersive virtual worlds, new ways of using crypto to facilitate club membership, concert tickets and company ownership. Every major tech company was proclaiming, planning, spending. To say nothing of brands, all eager to understand how to monetize the cryptoverse and to claim land. And VC companies with their seemingly limitless coffers, sprinkling their capital liberally across hundreds of new companies – over $33 billion in 2022 from 200 funds. The phrase 'Cambrian Period' immediately sprung to mind. A somewhat overused cliché that has been applied promiscuously, across wide swaths of historical observation. Fertile periods of innovation in technology, finance, political systems, science, arts or culture have often found themselves draped with this pithy phrase by one commentator or another. It is an easy borrow from the study of evolution; descriptive and vigorous.

One of the more concise definitions of the original Cambrian Period is 'the time when most of the major groups of animals first appear in the fossil record'. It was a remarkably short period, at least when compared to the history of life, which is around 3.8 billion years, give or take. The explosion of life forms during the Cambrian Period took place during a tiny sliver of this time, a mere fifty-five million years.

The startling new innovations and their impact discussed in this book are less than fifteen years old. A Cambrian Period indeed.

And what has flowered within this period has been the undisciplined and wildly mutating offspring of modern cryptography, whose underlying plumbing was built by a subcult of researchers, programmers, mathematicians and amateur sleuths. Their labours birthed a revolution in 2009, and from that time on we have seen a truly dizzying array of both successful and failed experimentation that has captured the attention of everyone – tech heads, central banks, legislators, mainstream media, curious onlookers, aspirant participants and all manner of grifters.

Cryptography – the mathematics of secret-keeping. It's been around for thousands of years, but of interest to us is the period fuelled by the release of the 2008 'whitepaper' entitled 'Bitcoin: A Peer-to-Peer Electronic Cash System', by the pseudonymous Satoshi Nakamoto, aided and informed by the aforementioned enthusiastic set of crypto-tinkerers stretching back to the 1970s.

And so, the blinking baby of Satoshi – the Bitcoin blockchain, and the subsequent supernovae of siblings and cousins and inbreeds, replete with bewildering new nicknames and monikers – cryptotokens, Defi, NFTs, the metaverse, Web3, DAOs, DIDs, soulbound tokens.

These wild and woolly new creatures were quickly staggering to their feet and knocking over long-established norms, but it was clear to me that something deeper was fuelling all of this energy. It was only partially to do with the much trumpeted features of public blockchain – decentralization, immutability, permissionlessness, trustlessness and the other shiny and somewhat arcane features of blockchains. Of course those were and are key to understanding the benefits of the underlying technology engine. But to me the blur of new blockchain projects and the parallel emergence of loud and bitter argument and insult in and around these new cryptofauna was camouflage for something more disruptive.

Books, blogs, podcasts, news outlets and courses offer how-tos and how-it-works and social impact analyses and economic musings and political filters about everything crypto. Social media overflows with commentary and contestation. We hear about the money-making opportunities and the displacement of ossified industries and sclerotic processes. But what is less apparent in all this cacophony is the *individual*, the citizen, the human at the end of the technology chain. You and me. And how our prospective immersion in these new technologies provides for something more personal and unprecedented.

And that is no less that the redefinition of the meaning of ownership in all its facets – identity, privacy, title, claim and transfer. And the rights and responsibilities attached to an individual who owns something.

Lest 'ownership' strike the reader as abstract, legal, even boring, consider this – it sits at the centre of civilization. It has been fuel for anger, jealousy, rage, wars, wealth, pride, peace, divorce, security and poverty since the beginning of humanity. There are people who own things and people who want to own those things. Either there is a peaceful transfer of ownership, or... theft, fraud, misappropriation, violence.

It could well be argued that we are what we own. At one time this was animals, wives, slaves, weapons, land, food. And then further up civilization's chain – cars, houses, jewellery, stocks, bonds, art, books, cutlery, Nikes, tickets, shares, voting rights, our right to our bodily autonomy. Our lives are adorned with the things we own. In many ways, they define us.

Every new blockchain-based project, in every industry, across every genre sits on this foundation – the ability for something to be owned publicly or privately without dispute, and as a caveat, the ability for owned items to be bought, sold, lent or borrowed instantaneously on frictionless markets at fair value.

In this book we will take a look at this wide new landscape through this overarching prism of dynamic, elastic and non-counterfeitable ownership. A look closely at this progeny of blockchain:

- NFTs have blazed a sensational trail through digital art and are beginning to tread on more conservative territories. NFTs, by definition, provide a secure title deed to a digital or even physical object, potentially infinite in its rules, but immutably tied to an owner.
- Decentralized Finance – Defi – previously a playground of the most adventurous and technologically sophisticated of money-jugglers, is now starting to gain wider acceptance. At its core, the ability for the individual to create and own their own journey with their own money through the world of finance without delegating the task to the rent-extraction of banks, centralized exchanges and other middlemen.
- Decentralized Autonomous Organizations – DAOs – are starting to challenge the traditional codifications of long-held formal structures that define everything from corporations to clubs, allowing individual participants to assemble, write and change their own rules of engagement.
- The metaverse – originally a creation of science fiction, has seen tens of billions of dollars of risk money pour into its coffers, its promise also fuelled by the potential of personal ownership of items and its associated property rights within its infinite imagined worlds. Detractors observe that this is not new. But blockchain changes the metaverse ecosystem.
- And of course, the OG: cryptocurrencies – no longer new or exotic, now that countries have started adopting them as legal tender, and governments have increasingly resigned themselves to their continued existence and beginning the process of building regulatory frameworks, forcing them, finally, to deal with privately owned money.
- Web3 – an in-process 'next' Internet, is now nailing down

its boundaries, at the centre of which is individual and immutable ownership of our personal interactions with the larger Internet ecosystem, giving us control of who may access, view, buy, sell our data, and under what conditions.

As we consider this personalized view of the growing crypto-economy and its many offshoots, we will also want to look at headwinds. Every new technology brings with it new opportunities for malfeasance, black swans, unintended consequences and painful shifts of power. A rewriting of the rules of ownership driven by cryptography is no exception – the headlines are already filled with dire warnings, misinformation, regulatory overreach and sensational stories of fraud and hucksterism. We need to dive in there too, and try to separate fact from fiction.

Most importantly, at least from my perspective, is how much fun this is. To return to our cliché borrowed from geological time – we are watching the evolution of a trans-formative techno-societal change in real-time. As long as we avoid the easy distractions of vast fortunes being made, lost or stolen, this is turning out to be a profoundly important human story.

And also, at the risk of repetition, *so* much fun to watch.

Explanatory Note

THE SHORTEST EXPLANATION OF BLOCKCHAIN YOU WILL EVER READ, WITH ALMOST NO JARGON

I resisted this. There are thousands and thousands of very good books and videos and podcasts and other online material about what a blockchain is and how it works. I didn't want readers to get bogged down in this before we entered the more important world of ownership. But it must be done, because at least some will want a recap or even a first look. But I promise you that you can skip this introductory chapter if you want.

The following is an explanation of the Bitcoin blockchain specifically, but most other blockchains are similar in principle.

I will do the what first, and the why after.

What is the Bitcoin blockchain?

- The blockchain is a database which contains a list of all Bitcoin payment transactions since its inception up until now.
- It is replicated on thousands of computers who are unknown to each other, but if a majority agree that they are looking at the identical database, then that is the one definitive version

of the truth. That makes it difficult to cheat, except with a prohibitively expensive coordinated effort to gain more than 50% colluding computers.

- The list is divided into blocks of Bitcoin transactions that have happened between individual account holders. Like I give you ten Bitcoins. Then you give someone else five Bitcoins. And so on. There are about 2,000 transactions in each block in the blockchain.

- Why blocks? Because it is easier to deal with than one long, never-ending stream of individual transactions; blocks are much more convenient.

- Blocks of transactions are assembled in near real time and added to the end of the database as transactions are continually requested by account holders.

- Each block is irrevocably mathematically chained to the previous history of blocks, all the way back to the very first Bitcoin transaction in 2010. Which means that no one can go back and change a transaction in history to their advantage, because the 'chain' of blocks is mathematically unbreakable. If someone tried, the mathematics would sound deafening klaxons and the attempt would be rejected.

- Each account holder is identified by a number only. No names.

- Only an account holder can withdraw and transfer their Bitcoins. Impossible for anyone else. Because the mathematics won't allow it (we will explain this in more detail later in the book).

- You cannot spend more than you have; the database calculates the current tally of savings of all account holders.

- It is impossible to spend the same Bitcoin twice – each transaction is time-stamped.

- The special computers doing the work of assembling blocks to keep it all in sync and operating are incentivized to do so using a little gift of Bitcoins from the blockchain. They are called miners. Thousands of other computers verify the miners' work. Only one miner assembles each block.

Why is any of this important?

- Because it means any account holder can pay any other account holder without anything sitting in the middle checking an account ledger (like a big bank computer that checks your balance before transferring money). This makes it fast and cheap and not reliant on trusting a bank.
- Because no one knows who is paying and who is being paid. Remember, no names, only numbers. Account holders keep their privacy.
- Because anyone can use it, no matter how rich or poor, documented or not, and be treated equally. This is not true of banks (try opening a bank account if you only have $20). It is the most inclusive monetary system in history.
- Because mathematics makes the whole enterprise impossible to change or cheat.
- Because there are no powerful humans anywhere in the system who can change anything or make questionable decisions (like printing more Bitcoin) beyond what is encoded in the system, it runs autonomously without managers, boards of directors or governments.

Yes, but really, why is this important?

Because the only other monetary system that has these properties is physical cash. And that is not your money. It is the government's money. And they can print more, inflate it, debase it, or take it back (history teems with examples, including right now). And a cash transaction is relatively slow to conclude (both parties must be physically present, you take it out of your pocket, hand it over, wait for change), it is subject to theft and loss, it is pretty useless across national borders and it is bulky to store in large amounts.

The blockchain fixes all of that.

Replace 'Bitcoin' with 'Cryptotoken', and this same explanation covers much wider territory.

That's really about it, save for a zillion details and decades of research and development.

Chapter I

OWNERSHIP AND ITS DISCONTENTS

> *Ownership is a massive vessel, freighted with implication, swayed by legal currents, caught in the conceptual eddies that whirl around every use of the possessive – 'my child', 'my house', 'my story', 'my body', 'my land', 'my language.'*
> Eula Biss

I love this description. I particularly love the repetitive simplicity of her use of that possessive 'my'. In thinking about the overarching subject of ownership I took an unavoidable trip to various thesauri. It turns out that there are very few synonyms for ownership. If I own it, it's mine. Not much more explanation needed.

Eula Biss is an award-winning non-fiction writer who, in 2020, wrote a book called *Having and Being Had*,[1] in which she ruminates on her discomfort at having just bought her first house. While trying to fill the house with stuff, she analyses our desire to own things, to possess. She questions whether this is not ruinous to our humanity, warping our attention that could be better spent elsewhere, like on human relationships.

I suspect she may be right, but the 'massive vessel' of ownership has been a constant companion of our species (and other species) for much of evolutionary history, and this book argues that it is on the precipice of redefinition, and perhaps even reimagination.

Once, when I was a skinny fourteen-year-old, a bunch of similar-aged friends had been given our first opportunity by our generous parents to go on holiday without them or any other adult. Rooms were booked at a hotel by the sea, we were given some spending money, instructed to call home every few days and delivered to the railway station, where we joyously boarded a train to the coast. To swim, to lie in the sun, to drink illicitly, perhaps to procure a joint or two, perhaps even to lose our virginity (which actually happened to my friend Brian, but not to me).

One of the little gifts from my mother for our oh-so-grown-up outing was a pair of sunglasses, expensive, branded, with a fancy little leather case. I had stared at myself in the mirror for many nights before we left, looking like a dashing aviator, I imagined. I would be irresistible to the objects of my desire, of that I was sure. God, I loved those sunglasses. It was my prized possession.

On the train my friends and I were in a sleeper cabin. Soon after we left, we met the residents of the next cabin. Older boys. From the wrong side of town. Big boys. Tough boys. They adopted us younger boys, and we wreaked havoc with noise and cigarettes and music. I was, of course, wearing my aviators, seeking to impress.

Which disappeared sometime during the night. And the leather case, which was on my sleeper bunk. Only to reappear on the acne-mottled face of the biggest tough a few hours later.

'Oh,' I said, 'you've borrowed my sunglasses.'

'Nah,' he said with threatening demeanour, 'these are mine.'

And that was that. I will return to this sad tale of ownership transfer, and the threat of violence that supported it, in a moment, but first we must take a short journey into human history. When did we first 'own' stuff? And who gave us permission to do so? And how did we prove it? There is an Alexandria's library worth of research, opinion and fact on this subject. Splayed across disciplines, from law to anthropology to sociology to history to business.

The whole concept of ownership is not that hard to understand, at least on the surface. We have all seen a domestic dog growl at an encroachment on its food. Similarly, we have seen animals share food with offspring. Even more convincing to watch is small children, toddlers perhaps (including my own, some time back). If you've ever watched the bawling, choking, puce-faced expression of infinite injustice and pain when one sibling seizes the toy of the other, or the sweet sharing of a piece of cake cementing the bonds of affection, then it is easy to see how fundamental ownership is to our sense of morality and community and our understanding of possession.

And the codification of ownership, whose expression is so naturally evident in animals and children, has been an accompaniment to human societies for a very long time, at least since the time humans learned to write, and likely before.

One of more interesting frameworks to slide across my screen was by Tilman Hartley, a sociologist from the University of Bristol, in a paper entitled 'The Continuing Evolution of Ownership'[2] and which offers a fairly unique taxonomy as a scaffold. He posits this – first there was the initial OG, selfish ownership (or, more politely, first possession). Claiming a natural resource as your own. As in – Hey! That's my rock! Give it back before I club you over the head!

Then there was community ownership (shared resources among a clan of common interest, like the need for sustenance).

Then there was hierarchical (or command) ownership, with crumbs doled out for the rest of us (imposed by monarchs, religious leaders, landed gentry, lineage, etc).

And finally there was title ownership (the ownership space where most of us live, where documents give relative certainty and security to owned possessions).

Tilman digs deeply into the tensions of communal, command and title ownership, sketching out the dynamics of different actors and actions – Demanders, Resisters and Transferrers – which are considerably different in each category. You can imagine the fun you might have challenging the king who has just commandeered your favourite horse vs the relative ease with which you can replace a stolen credit card.

There is a deep exposition in this paper uncovering the reasons for these types of ownership, tethered closely to the evolution of hominids and human societies. For instance, sharing was an ideal strategy when big game was abundant and the clan needed to be kept healthy in order to be able to defend itself against outsiders.

Later, when the game started to be hunted out and agriculture started to provide food security, communities became more sedentary and class stratification (greed, I suppose) started to take hold. There is apparently evidence of this as far back as 29,000 years ago, although it became much clearer about 12,000 years ago in Asia, where small villages and nuclear families emerged. Those with power (usually physical) and motive were able to own outsized slices of the 'luxury' pie (shelter, food, animals, women, weapons) and shave off the bare minima for the lower classes to survive and do their bidding. Lest we think those days are long gone, there will be those that argue that capitalism is simply a softer implementation of this. And for those in command economies like North Korea, it is a brutal everyday reality.

Moving on (before we fall hopelessly into the abyss of class politics), there was the emergence of 'title' ownership. Title is a loose term, but for our purposes let's just define it as proof of ownership, documented and attested by some authority (these last two words are profoundly freighted in the world of crypto as we will see, in which the words 'some authority' will be replaced by 'mathematics'). In any event, Tilman's literature review points to the likely emergence of title about 5,500 years ago in Mesopotamia, where clay tablets were used for the purpose. And then a long line of title innovations – land, houses, loans, goods, identity. Memorialized on clay, papyrus, paper with stamps, seals, oaths and signatures. And the emergence of trusted third parties to attest to and take custody of those titles (and to be paid for that service) – banks, lawyers, governments, commercial databases, trusts.

And of course, title self-custody, ending up with all sorts of documents which I have a terrible time storing in a properly retrievable form, both physical or digital. (One look at my filing system on Dropbox quickly reminds me of my limitations, not to mention the old metal filing cabinet in the corner where things were once classified and alphabetized and now moan in chaos). As for the rest – the stuff held by banks and lawyers and municipal and national authorities, well, I simply give my trust over, notwithstanding a never-ending stream of scary headlines of demand, seizure, loss and theft.

We could go deeper, foraging around in the actual deeds and documents and declarations, but for our purposes this is what we need to know. We have ownership codifications in our lives. Mostly for the big stuff – wills (instructions for transfer), houses (title deeds), cars (registration documents), birth certificates and passports (identity), licences (authorizations to act), warranty deeds, quitclaims, etc. And then further on down the value chain – receipts, invoices, payment records.

Let us consider circumstances in which there is no record of provenance or ownership at all, and the mischief that can ensue, which takes us back to the tale of my lost sunglasses and my impotence in resisting that transfer of ownership. Via Tilman's lens I had been brutalized by category 2 of his taxonomy. The unquestioned rights of hierarchical power and command ownership, enforced by a threat of violence. Without a title deed, it was over. And my similarly cowardly friends were not going to be courageous enough to threaten counter-violence on my behalf.

Which brings me to a similar but much larger anecdote. The second-largest blockchain is called Ethereum, worth hundreds of billions of dollars. Not yet a household name like Bitcoin, but known to millions and doing yeoman's service in myriad applications. We will get into its secret sauce later in the book, but its godhead is a skinny Russian-Canadian by the name of Vitalek Buterin. Not pseudonymous like Satoshi Nakamoto, but very much alive and visible and constantly in the news.

He was deep into gaming as a kid, from 2007 to 2010. A game called *World of Warcraft* was his preference. The company behind it was called Blizzard, which still exists as a subsidiary of Activision. One day, they changed the rules of the game and Vitalek's favourite warlord lost one of his most important powers, his 'life spell'. Simply taken away. Vitalek says, 'I cried myself to sleep that night.'

One could hypothesize that he went on to create one of the second-most important blockchain innovations in history to make sure this never happened again (he himself argues that this was the spark), but a more important matter lies buried beneath this story. Vitalek was spoofed into thinking that his videogame character and its special powers wouldn't be taken away. It was. It belonged to someone else, and they did exactly that. He had no recourse at all. He has no way even to pay market value for a transfer of ownership of the life spell, now so cruelly denied to him and his warlord. He had no idea of the terms of Blizzard's centralized ownership of the life spell (and everything else in the game), and it never struck him to ask Blizzard because, well, who would think of doing that?

Vitalek has written that it was centralization that was at the root of his pain and that decentralization (a key feature of public blockchains) was the cure. Of course. But I contend the deeper heart of his misery was a misunderstanding of the nature of who owned what and what they could do with their rights.

We go one further. Satoshi Nakamoto, the person who wrote the Bitcoin whitepaper, supposedly owns about one million Bitcoins. That value makes Satoshi one of the richest people in the world. He (or she or they) has never spent any of it or moved any of it. The owner(s) may be dead or alive. But the provenance of the ownership of the wallets that have all of those Bitcoins is available for anyone to inspect. Here is his original account number (derived from what is called a public key) on the Bitcoin blockchain: 1A1zP1eP5QGefi2DMPTfTL5SLmv7DivfNa – although he had many more, perhaps thousands. Anybody can see what's in there, and track where it came from – it takes even a non-technical observer a few seconds. It cannot be rifled, moved, disputed or seized by anyone but the owner, including a government.

It is irrevocably and immutably owned. Under possession until further notice.

Let's now take a look at a title deed for a house, and how one acquires it or transfers it. The pain I am about to mete out to you is based on the processes in the country in which I now reside (South Africa), but I have also owned houses on other continents, including the US, and it is not dissimilar there. I apologize in advance – avert your eyes if need be.

This then, from one of the websites dedicated to title deeds (this one called Ooba):

- A description of the property, with its size, boundaries and exact position.
- The name and identity number of the person or persons who legally own the property (it is possible for more than one owner to be listed on a title deed).
- The date when the property was last transferred.
- If bought from another person, the purchase price.
- Any factors that could restrict the sale of the property, for example, a home loan.
- Any restriction that applies on the purchase of the property. For example, the title deed should state if the property has a full freehold title.
- An official Deeds Registry Office seal to indicate that the deed has been recorded in the name of the owner and the date.

All house title deeds look similar to this. You may not add some wishful fancy of your own, like – 'I want my wife to own the property every alternate week'. I repeat, you cannot easily construct an exclusion of your own. The title deed is largely inflexible. And I love the requirement for an official registry office seal. You know, one of those mechanical things that you apply hand pressure to so that a corner underlying document becomes indented with little pits and bubbles that are supposed to mean something. One wonders how long that has been used, and whether anyone thinks that this represents clever security.

And it gets worse. Let's say you want to buy a house. And thus have a title deed transferred to your name, so that you may later transfer it to someone else, at your discretion. Firstly someone (you or your agent or someone else) has to check the existing title deed. In order to do this, here is the process:

- Go to any deeds office (deeds registries may not give out information acting on a letter or a telephone call).
- Go to the information desk, where an official will help you complete a prescribed form and explain the procedure.
- Request a data typist to search for the property, pay the required fee at the cashier's office and take the receipt back to the official at the information desk.
- The receipt number will be allocated to your copy of the title.

Is anyone losing their will to live yet? Oh, wait, there is an online version provided by the South African government called DeedsWeb where you can interact with deeds. Here is what you need *just to register for the site*:

- Copy of identity document
- Proof of residence

- Three months' statements of two credit references
- Banking details (copy of bank statement or cancelled cheque)
- Registration document (for a company)
- Fidelity certificate (if applicable)
- Consent letter (for a company), if it has more than one director
- It takes forty-eight hours to get registered. And this is the electronic version. In 2022.

OK, I'm going to stop here, and I haven't even got to the deed transfer process. I hope the point is made. Title ownership under a regime of pre-blockchain technologies is, well, Dickensian (to stretch a metaphor), even when things are digital. One may argue that, for other, less valuable objects, deeds of ownership or transfer documents are simpler – car registrations, wills, bills-of-sale, passports, drivers' licences. No, not really. As anyone who has lost one of these documents can attest.

Furthermore, the cost of title ownership is non-trivial. In the example above, no one in their right minds would attempt to claw through the house title registration and title transfer tangle alone. There is a layer of middlemen who handle what is euphemistically called the details – agents, lawyers, local government bureaucrats. All of whose fees end up being paid by either the buyer or seller. Even in the best of circumstances, a somewhat bewildering and dispiriting process.

There are other examples I might have chosen to illustrate this point about the outdated, convoluted and near-extortionate costs of traditional title regimes. But houses are apposite. Because of what happened last year.

On the 8th of February 2022, a real-estate company called Propy announced that they had just facilitated the sale of the first home in the US using an NFT, one of the blockchain-borne creatures we will discuss later, to secure the ownership. The 2,164 square foot home has 4 bedrooms, 3.5 bathrooms and is located at 6315 11th Avenue South, Gulfport, FL 33707. The home was on auction and the winning bid was 210 ETH (ETH is a cryptocurrency), valued at $654,309.60 at the time of sale.

So this all looks very impressive indeed. The NFT, which we will get into later, is lodged on the Ethereum blockchain, immutably and cryptographically tethered to an owner who can choose to sell it later to anyone at their discretion.

Game over, right? Is all the title nastiness described in previous paragraphs a thing of the past?

No, unfortunately. At least not yet. Local laws and policies regarding title registration have not changed, and neither are they likely to do so for some time, given the torpid pace of legislative and policy change. So all that work described earlier still had to be done. The real change was the currency used to settle the bill of sale, and the immutable NFT that is glued to that house, acting just like a title deed, stronger, better, more flexible and more accessible than the old one, but not in the eyes of the mandarins of Tampa Bay, who will still insist on the old way.

In October 2022, a $175,000 South Carolina home was sold by a company called Roofstock via NFT, doing an end-run around the mandarins by having a Limited Liability Company owning the house and then applying the NFT sales to the LLC, not the house. Quite clever, but not quite the same thing as an individual buying a house.

But it's a start. At some point (soon, I predict), some forward-looking tech-savvy city alderman will look at NFT-secured properties and say – what in the world do we need those old, cumbersome titles for? NFTs are far better title deeds, blockchain-secured and transferred automatically by code the moment the buyer deposits crypto in the seller's wallet. Then he or she will spin up a PowerPoint presentation at the next city council meeting, which will say things like 'reduction of time from months to seconds' and 'secure and immutable and instantaneous access and traceability' and 'counterfeit-resistance' and the flexibility to include fanciful conditions like 'my wife owns it every alternate week' and, and. He or she will face derision and eye-rolling, and then he or she will try again the next month, and the next, and then one day the council will agree and pitch it to the state legislature, and then...

* * *

Early in 2021 a book was published called *Mine!: How the Hidden Rules of Ownership Control Our Lives.*[3] The book was written by authors and professors James Salzman (UCLA Law School) and Michael Heller (Columbia Law School). The book does not drift into a discussion about crypto and its connection to ownership at all – perhaps because of its timing and regulatory uncertainty – but is an expansive, authoritative, generous and entertaining sweep across the entire universe of ownership, particularly where it upends our intuitive understanding of the term, and some of the porous borders and unintended consequences of possession, and how the things that we own, or think that we own, sometimes end up in a confusion of competing claims and interests.

And so the pages are chock-full of the most riveting, occasionally amusing, occasionally tragic of human stories, all illustrating the surprising societal shapeshift of the ownership story. Do you 'own' the spot in the concert queue for which you have paid someone to stand? Do you 'own' the right to reserve a seat for a tardy friend at an open seating when everyone else has turned up to an event on time? Do you 'own' the space between your knees and the airplane seat which may recline and remove that space? How long can you own a copyright? When does copyright protection actually become counterproductive for the public good? Is the drone above the home that you own a trespasser? The water table underneath? Who owns the spit that you sent 23andMe for DNA testing? What happens when inherited land is passed down from generation to generation until there are thousands of claimants?

While fascinating examples like these spill out of every chapter, they form the specific examples that support a general scaffold, somewhat different than Tilman Hartley's scaffold described earlier in this chapter. The scaffold presented by the authors is expressed as an ownership toolkit – *first-in-time, possession, labour, attachment, self-ownership and family*. But in clever riddling that foreshadows the counter-intuitiveness of the many of our perceptions of the ownership story, the chapters are instead titled – *First Come, Last Served; Possession Is One-Tenth Of The Law; I Reap What You Sow, My Home Is Not My Castle, Our Bodies, Not Ourselves, The Meek Shall Inherit Very Little*.

The book wanders promiscuously through many territories – the way that owners can bend and manipulate the world to their intents, the way that even those who think that they own things end up finding definitions to be squishy; and the difference between governing laws of ownership, the regulations that try to enforce them, and the shakiness of implementation details – which of course, leads straight back to the courts, who play King Solomon in the face of ambiguity.

Crypto and its expression on the blockchain, even given the heft and change that it will bring to many aspects of ownership, is not going to make a difference to every matter discussed in their book. As the authors state, 'ownership is the scaffolding that society uses to structure every struggle over the things we all want'. Given the fact that we all want somewhat different things, particularly as you look across cultures and worldviews, those 'struggles' cannot always be codified into laws that are precise or fair enough to satisfy everyone.

I will argue that the new injection of crypto into the ownership story will be transformative in ways that are profoundly important to our future as a society. But we are human, and because of that, the edges of ownership will never be perfectly defined.

Chapter 2

SECRETS AND THE MATHEMATICS OF OWNERSHIP, LIGHTLY TOLD

This chapter sets itself a high hurdle. It is about the mathematics of secrets and how that informs and secures ownership. But it has no aspiration to try and describe the maths in anything even approaching rigour. So it will, as far as possible, strive for metaphor and analogy and eschew the arcane symbology of maths.

Those readers who are aware of some of the gnarlier details of both the maths and how it is expressed on the blockchain will find me skating on very thin ice occasionally. It is done on purpose, favouring simplicity above precision.

We start with secrets. In 1999 a book called *The Code Book: The Science of Secrecy from Ancient Egypt to Quantum Cryptography*,[4] by famed English popular science writer Simon Singh, was published. It was about the history of secrets and how humanity has engineered techniques to keep them. All the way back from the need to keep them (which stretches back through human history to the earliest societies) to some of the newest and most startling developments in cryptography of the time. It was published almost ten years before Satoshi's whitepaper birthed the blockchain, but its revelations are apposite and still relevant, and one of its chapters is the core of what now underlies blockchain cryptography. That this book was written far earlier than Satoshi's whitepaper demonstrates that the original blockchain and everything that came after was made with *existing* toolsets, *existing* maths – it is the way the ecosystem was imagined, designed and deployed which made it revolutionary.

The human need to keep secrets does not require an academic treatise, although there are those. As in the previous chapter, just observe children. They keep secrets to themselves (often for self-preservation – revealing secrets about the empty cookie jar might bring unwelcome circumstances) or they share secrets with favoured parties, like a sibling or friend. And they sometimes fail to keep them, through malice or error, under threat or for strategy. (These last four nouns are important. It covers the entire spectrum of sensational news reports around cryptotoken mischief and loss.)

But secrets take on a much more freighted complexion when there is money or influence or even lives at stake. Singh, in an early example in the book, takes us to ancient battlefields, where generals needed to communicate tactics to field commanders without the enemy finding out. Huge stakes here, perhaps the fate of nations. And a straight line from there to here, where we, as citizens and individuals spend what seems like an inordinate amount of time on everything from clever hiding places for keys, to cumbersome safes for jewellery, to passwords for the digital world, to external custodians like banks and lawyers to keep our secrets from revelation and misappropriation. While the darker forces of theft, fraud, seizure and greed lurk nearby, always seeking to steal secrets for profit.

The history of the battle between secret keepers and secret stealers is a thriller. A book plot in itself, perhaps, fiction-like in its dramatic narratives, within fearful innocents and predators at its heart.

Secrets. Everything starts here, and the whole massive churning crypto enterprise rests on this kernel – it allows participants to keep secrets which leads directly to mathematically secure and counterfeit-proof titles for the first time in human history. At the risk of using this hammer too obviously, here are a few simple examples of the direct relationship between secrets and ownership.

Let's say you have a lockbox in your home (a rather quaint concept these days), within which are kept some old but sentimentally important family heirlooms. You have a key for the lockbox and you hide that key by cleverly taping it under the drawer next to your bed. Every now and then you open the box and gaze at the objects. It brings you pleasure, you have no thought of profit, even though the heirlooms might be valuable, and will one day leave these objects to your descendants.

A number of things can go wrong with this scheme that ensures your ownership of the objects in the box. You might share the key's location with a sibling. It is now not wholly and securely yours any more, there has been risk leakage, and now that ownership is dependent on human trust, a famously unreliable state of affairs. You must now rely on your sibling's better nature, which you have never questioned, but you never know in this world.

You might forget where you hid the key (who among us has not forgotten where the clever hiding place was?). In this case, your ownership of the objects is all for nought – you have lost access. You could smash the box open of course, but then your ownership was never secured by the secret of the key's location in the first place.

The key or lock might get damaged, leaving you unable to get into the box. A rare but occasional occurrence in real life too.

These examples may seem trivial, but your secret knowledge of where the key is, and the secure interaction of the key, lock and box is the entire ownership ecosystem.

It doesn't stop there. Let's say you want to share a secret with someone. To facilitate joint ownership. A trusted spouse perhaps, with whom you share the login details for your bank account. You have now doubled the attack surface of the control of your funds in your bank – the bad guys now have two people from whom to try and steal instead of one. And if you emailed the login details – hoo boy – your attack surface expanded in more ways than is comfortable to contemplate.

There is an important nuance to consider here. The secret (location of the key or the makeup of the username/password) does two important things for the owner. It confirms that the person in possession of the secret is the rightful owner of the stuff (because the key unlocks). And it confers *access* to the owned stuff. These are two distinct matters, which will have bearing on the cryptographic core of blockchain.

A pause here. Do we actually need to have a secret to own something? No, we don't, but it helps to secure that ownership. Confirmation of ownership traditionally swirls around some combination of three factors. Something you know (a secret, like a password), something you have (like an access card or physical item like a driver's licence) and something you are (a biometric, like a fingerprint). Only the first one of those factors is in the business of secrets. The identification of your face on your iPhone is not a secret. It is pretty public and it can't be faked. But the blockchain is based on the private revelation of a secret to its internal mathematics, so let's keep moving.

In the previous book that I co-authored with Simon Dingle, we gave a simple algebraic example to illustrate a mathematical oddity called a trapdoor function. I got yelled at by someone who had had the bare minimum of mathematics in high school, so let me try again. A trapdoor function is a sort of mathematical 'equation' that is really easy to compute in one direction, but not the other. What does 'direction' mean?

A simple illustrative example should make this obvious. If I ask you to multiply two prime number together, like 7x13, it is a trivial exercise. You could do it in your head fairly easily, perhaps with a little trickery like first multiplying 7x12 and then adding 7 to give the solution of 91. But suppose I had asked you to find me the two largest prime numbers that, when multiplied together give an answer of 91, then you would have to work much harder to find the solution. That is what is meant by trivial in one direction but hard in the other. A heap of maths brings us a set of mathematical 'functions' which are computationally trivial in one direction, but very difficult the other way. How difficult you might ask? Well, nearly impossible. The phrase 'prohibitively expensive' is often used. So difficult that mathematicians replace the equal sign by a little sign that looks a little like a one-way arrow. The trapdoor function is one of those.

What is the relevance to our story? I'm jumping over a whole slew of details here, but it makes it impossible for anyone but the owner to move money out of their account, but easy for anyone to move money into an account or just to take a peek as to what is in there. It makes it impossible for any actor to go back and change an historical entry in the blockchain, but trivial to check that a new incoming entry is valid. These statements are so key to the soul of blockchain they bear repeating. The trapdoor function has enabled the building of a technical system that makes it impossible to cheat the system but trivial to verify validity (or 'truthiness'). Or, alternatively, hard to forge a message, but easy to verify who signed it. This all-critical 'digital' signature, fed by the one-way function, has led some commentators to define a blockchain as nothing more than a chain of digital signatures.

This little mathematical oddity (and its close cousin the 'one-way function') is the nuclear core of almost everything in modern crypto – it is the deep moat that has enabled cryptographers to mount a (so far) impenetrable defence against cybercriminals and hackers trying to break into the blockchain (and in the case of Bitcoin, they have been trying for 13 years). The trapdoor function, once it had been beaten into mathematical submission by a cadre of smart research-ers, became the fuel for the two sentries of the blockchain.

Who are they?

I jumped directly from the trapdoor function to its impact on an account sitting on a blockchain, and purposefully left out the weighty centre – these two sentries – public/private key pairs and the hash function. But, as it says in the chapter heading, this chapter is lightly told. So it will be.

Each 'account' on the blockchain is connected to a unique pair of keys, called the private key and the public key, which are themselves squeezed out of the maths behind the trapdoor function. The owner of the account holds the private key. Which is sort of like a password, a secret known only to them. That 'secret' is the key to popping back through the 'trapdoor', and allowing withdrawal and transfer of cryptotokens. No one who is not in possession of the private key can do this – they are stuck on the other side of the trapdoor. The public key, on the other hand, which is uniquely and mathematically glued to that unique private key, is available to anyone. It allows them to direct transfers of cryptotokens *into* the owner's account, and to know with certainty who the owner of an account is. The hash, another clever mathematical creature, ensures that participants in the blockchain can hide the details of their messages, even though those messages can be verified as valid. If this sounds like magic, it sort of is.

Anyone with knowledge of blockchain mechanics will know that in striving for simplicity I am leaving out a mountain of details and skirting on the edges of technical accuracy, but the core principle is all that is required here – authorized parties securely send and receive self-owned cryptotokens to and from each other, without the intervention, surveillance and facilitation of any third party, the whole shebang secured by a mathematical secrets.

Which brings us to the story of James H. Ellis, a story which is simultaneously glorious and sad. He was born in Australia in September 1924, but grew up in England. He was beset with multiple early misfortunes – he nearly died at birth, his caregivers thought he was learning-disabled and he was an early orphan. Hard to come back from all of that.

But he did, excelling at maths in school, getting a degree in physics, getting married, having four children and entering the British civil service, where he worked comfortably as an engineer and mathematician, ending up at the Communications Electronics Security Group in 1965 after a number of other government posts. If you haven't heard of this place, don't be surprised. It operated somewhat in the shadows, much of its work secret because some of it was tied to Britain's military and national security, and much of it became classified. Secret enough that Ellis's wife and kids apparently had no idea what he did all day.

He took this secrecy very seriously. He played by the rules in a time when (at least in my somewhat rose-tinted remembrance of history) labouring in the public service was seen as a privilege. If your government said 'don't tell anyone', you didn't.

So he laboured in obscurity, satisfied with his contribution to his country. And he wrote a paper in 1969 which should have earned him a shining place in history; its contents helped to upend 3,000 years of civilization's technologies of privacy – the discovery of the private/public key pair. But because of the keep-quiet laws nobody except a small group of similarly taciturn researchers knew about it. In 1997, it was revealed that he had written the original paper. But Ellis also died in 1997. There was no time for him to get his dues and awards while he was alive. That breaks my heart.

In 1976, seven years after he wrote his still-embargoed paper, a different group of researchers, most prominently Whitfield Diffie and Martin Hellman, and (separately) Ralph Merkle, reinvented what Ellis had initially described, now widely known as asymmetric key cryptography, giving life to the very same public/private key technology (usually just called public key cryptography) that is used by all blockchains today, and the basis for much of the digital security industry outside of blockchains.

How important was Ellis's discovery?

During the Renaissance, a new and unprecedented method of encryption arose called polyalphabetic substitution. While the encryption scheme matured and changed over time, its base principles remained unchanged (replacing the letters of a written secret with letters from one or more alternative alphabets), and it was so efficient that German intelligence used a version of it in their famed Enigma encryption device. David Kahn is a historian who has written some of the most definitive books about the history of cryptography, including the seminal *The Codebreakers* in 1967[5]. His reaction to public-key cryptography, first understood and documented by Ellis, was 'the most revolutionary new concept in the field since polyalphabetic substitution emerged in the Renaissance'.

Diffie, Hellman and Merkle got the recognition for inventing a dazzling secrecy technique which is now at the core of a new trillion-dollar industry.

Ellis could only watch quietly as he kept his word to his government not to tell anyone. He never even got to see the development of the blockchain.

Chapter 3

TRUST NO ONE, LEST THEY TAKE WHAT IS YOURS

The word 'trust' is deeply embedded in the literature of crypto. And its derivative 'trustlessness', coined to describe one of the features of the blockchain. A bit confusing, that one. Sounds like it could be interpreted as 'having less trust', which spills easily over into 'not to be trusted'. But of course, its meaning sits elsewhere – you don't have to trust this thing, because it does not require any trust at all. Which in turns spills over into the oft-used homily 'don't trust, verify', with our mathematical function – the trapdoor function – stolidly offering its support services.

There is a reason for the search for trustlessness – where there is a need for trust, there is certain to be breaches of trust, particularly where humans are involved. It is embedded in our history; the smaller and larger gods of human betrayals and theft. The techno-philosophers behind crypto wanted to do better. They wanted to take trust entirely off the table as a mechanism of misdemeanour.

OK, so perhaps Satoshi and colleagues (or those cryptographers who had come before) had scarred childhoods damaged by theft. Or perhaps research had been done which concluded that trustees everywhere had enjoyed a long historical bacchanal of larceny. Or perhaps the industry of trusteeship was just too damn expensive. Who were these trustees and other similar middlemen? Custodians like lawyers and banks and brokers and accountants and registries. And the filing cabinets and hard disks everywhere which hold your titles and passwords that attest to our ownership of things.

I wanted to find out, so I set off in search of some answers, particularly with regards to two matters. How big is the world of trustees and middlemen who protect and transfer ownership on behalf of customers, and how much do they charge? The task bested me quite quickly. Partially because most of the actors I mention do other things besides taking temporary custody of stuff you own, so carving this out seems like an impossible task. But I got one hard figure from crypto luminary David Chaum (who we will meet soon). He threw it out in a podcast, but I can't trace the source, and will have to trust him – his reputation demands it. The fees we pay to global financial institutions to move our money around? $3 *trillion*. I am not talking about the profits raked in by banks on loans, etc. Just the fees. The one that appears in your statements, trying to hide embarrassedly at the bottom of the page. $3 trillion. One of those numbers big enough to have limited meaning.

I am rather hopeful that some student reader or two some-where will see this as fertile grounds for a PhD thesis – it seems to be an open research question. Where we would like to get to is a statement like this – trustees and middlemen who secure the custody and transfer of third-party owned stuff represent an industry of $xx, and charge $yy for their services. Then we at least would know the size of the industry that has a blockchain target on its back.

There is a lurking elephant in this discussion of middle-men, which I am going to pretend is not there, lest this book spin off into areas beyond its remit. But let me snapshot the beast, and then leave it hanging on the wall. We are making a case that the blockchain and crypto is changing the nature of ownership, and this chapter addresses the matter of trust and its demands. And so we must necessarily talk about trustees and middlemen.

And here is where the elephant takes shape. Columbia law professor Kathryn Judge has written a book called *Direct: The Rise of the Middleman Economy and the Power of Going to the Source*.[6] In it she describes the accretion of power around the largest of middlemen who dominate the supply chain (think Amazon), and how on the one hand they provide great convenience and choice, but on the other hand this comes at a price, given the startling techniques of 'influ-ence' that these companies have, not only on the competitive market, but because of their influence on you, the consumer. They harvest your data and shopping habits and use them to provide fodder for clever algorithms that will nudge you to buy this or that, tilting scales in their commercial interests, but not necessarily in yours.

In other words, the biggest and smartest of the middlemen have a pernicious influence on what you may wish to *buy* and own. And her fightback recommendation is to go to the source, as her subtitle proclaims. She is suggesting direct exchange between buyer and seller as a mechanism. Which brings us directly to our topic, the power of blockchain to exclude 'trusted' middlemen and their influence on the ownership. A breach of trust is not only a precursor to theft or misappropriation. It can also mean undue influence of what you seek to own. And so the elephant – the invidious algorithms of powerful middlemen that silently tell you what you should buy. To remove the trust you have surrendered to the middleman, you must remove the middleman, even if they have no intent to actually steal your stuff. Their interest may lie more in stealing your independence of choice.

Not to tar everyone with the same brush, there are of course many large supply-chain middlemen who are innocent of applying the dark arts of digital nudging, and who provide valuable services even as they take ownership of our assets for some short period of time. And then there are the others for whom these personal influence techniques are simply seen as smart business.

So we will leave that elephant alone. Back to my search for the size of the trustee and middleman business and how crypto-secured ownership will disrupt it.

I found this: trustees in Australia have custody of AU$500 billion of assets, both personal and institutional (this from an Australian Financial Services Council[7] report). This is about 25% of Australia's GDP.

I was astounded by this figure. If we extrapolate that (using some reckless high-school maths), then we must conclude that worldwide about $20 trillion dollars' worth of stuff is held in trust by people and entities who don't own it. And this is not the full picture of course: many other trustees are private and have no public record of the extent of their control. A lawyer perhaps, who holds custody of your assets without the public attestation of a registered trust.

Some prudence is advised here. Trustees of these massive amounts are almost entirely well-regulated, honest, efficient and necessary. They fulfil a role, a need that has arisen for all sorts of valid reasons, such as efficient financial structuring under regulatory mandate or for tax reasons. But it is not possible to extract what we pay for that trust. For instance, your accountant may have permission to transact on your behalf, but what percentage of their fees is applied to 'trusteeship'? Same with your bank, your lawyer. And that is because fees for trust are, quite simply, integrated into other services. You may have an *actual* legal trust company looking after stuff – that is an easier thing to quantify. But not with your family lawyer or the bank who arranges your credit card delivery.

So we pause our search for the size and cost of a sprawling service industry who protects and transfers ownership on behalf of others, other than to say it is large. But we can try to give the correct weight to this matter by simply looking at the average citizen. Or *homo confidens*, 'trusting man', if you will excuse the Google translate.

We are people who trust other people – there is no other way to live. We start with our mothers when we are born, and depending on the fates and furies, we extend our trust outwards, to family, to friends, to neighbours, to tribe, to creed, to colleagues, to strangers. And not always in that order, as depressing news headlines continually remind us.

It is in this process, as we grow from infancy to adulthood, that our trust gets tested and shaped. Luck, at least partially, is the great pruner of the trust tree. Cruel or neglectful parents, betrayals by friends, incidents of theft, arbitrary misfortune – all of these give shape to each individual's view of whom to trust and to what depth. So back to our *homo confidens*. He or she trusts their mother, their father, their two siblings, their surviving grandparents, their children. Oh, and their three best friends, but not all of their friends' spouses. At least not the one with the drinking problem. There is a pastor who they trust, a retired teacher from way back and a boss from a recent job. A doctor and their current lawyer, but not the previous one who made a costly error on a document. And the plumber, but not so much the electrician who overcharged. They trust the babysitter with the kids, but not with the car. They trust this friend with keeping a family secret but not with fashion advice.

And so on. Layers of trust, types of trust, depth of trust, shards of trust, conditional trust. We can live with that; it is the background to our human relationships, and its diversity gives colour and texture to our daily interactions and our internal understanding of risk.

And critically to our discussion, we know with certainty that this chaotic network of trust relationships is *dynamic*. It changes constantly. A trustworthy person disappoints, an untrustworthy one changes their ways. *Homo confidens* exists in a constantly shape-shifting world, and must remain vigilant at all times, watching for breaches and leakage, re-evaluating the trust network constantly.

Which is where we get to technology. The academic literature around this fizzes and pops. There is a wonderful paper called 'Understanding the creation of trust in cryptocurrencies: the case of Bitcoin'[8] which gets deep into the weeds, and provides helpful, if daunting, links to thirty years of academic research on trust.

There are a couple of pithy quotes from this article that bear repeating, such as 'Trust refers to the willingness of a party to be vulnerable to the actions of another party based on the expectation that the other party will perform an action important to the trustor, irrespective of the ability to monitor or control that other party' (R.C. Mayer).

Two things in this definition jumped out at me. The first was the word *vulnerability*, fraught with fear and innocence. That is us, trusting men and women, *homo confidens*, making ourselves vulnerable because we trust people, even though we know that some people can't be fully, completely and irrevocably trusted, even those people who once shone with it. In this matter we are just sitting ducks, waiting to get smacked around, forced to change our calculus when we do. Trust and vulnerability are conjoined twins.

The second was the phrase 'irrespective of the ability to monitor or control that other party' (the trustee). Indeed, none of us have the time or telemetry to monitor or control our trustees. Until it turns out they have done something bad. Sometimes we just give our trust over to them and cross our fingers. To banks. To governments. To brokers. Part with our secrets and our stuff and hope for the best, based often on no more than a signature and a promise and the hope that some authority down the road will make you whole when it all goes pear-shaped.

Another definition is 'It is an individual's reliance on another person under conditions of dependence and risk' (from a book edited by R. Kramer and T. Tyler).[9] Uh-huh. Tears, anger and courts at the end of this definition.

The authors take us by the hand and lead us from trusting humans to trusting technology with this interesting observation – '...if technology resembles the qualities of humans, then people trust technology'. It is interesting because the attributes of a trustworthy human are described as benevolence, integrity and ability. And their technological equivalents are described as helpfulness, reliability and functionality.

I am not sure I fully buy into this mapping, but no matter – there is clearly a somewhat different set of constructs that govern when we choose to trust humans vs when we choose to trust technologies. We can never really know humans; we rely on all manner of heuristics as a guide. We usually don't know technologies either (unless we are the builders), and we trust them until they break or underperform, and then we don't trust them any more. Perhaps we may end up suing the builders, but at least our hearts aren't broken.

Here comes the punchline. Our trust in humans can be misplaced, unjustified, poorly judged. It is not reliable, it is squishy. Our trust in tech requires only a failure of function to be broken. Not squishy at all, more precise, but still not trustworthy.

So who you are you going to trust?

Mathematics. This is not a surprise: it has been at the centre of the crypto proposition from the beginning. This is the magisterium from whence our trapdoor function hails.

Easy to agree with, but a little harder to tether to the subject at hand – how are you going to build a technology that expresses this mathematics in a reliable and trustworthy way?

Satoshi's whitepaper, which is not that difficult to read, and mercifully short (nine pages), is the expression of the maths into diagrams and English prose. Reading it is revelatory, it makes the heart beat a little faster. After he wrote it, a core group of developers, all colleagues of Satoshi (and now armed with the defining whitepaper) started programming and testing and fixing and swapping code and upgrading and retesting and moulding and pruning and retesting again until they had something that worked. That allowed participants to own and safely transfer a token to a counterparty without a middleman. And then they released that code to the world. In its entirety. To set fire to, to beat with a hammer, to roll over with a tank. Moreover, when the price of Bitcoin offered the chance of fortunes, no one, no matter how smart or well-funded, was able to find a chink anywhere.

I would argue that this makes this technology the most trustworthy ever invented by man, a perfect fit of form and function, an impregnable coat of armour for the keeping of secrets and the protection of possession.

Chapter 4

ASPIRATIONS OF THE SOVEREIGN INDIVIDUAL

In 1997, James Dale Davidson and Lord William Rees-Mogg wrote a book called *The Sovereign Individual*,[10] in which they described humanity's history as being formed by the threat of violence from centralized powers like nation-states, and foresaw all sorts of disruption and trouble ahead, including the wrenching and breaking apart of countries as law-abiding as Canada and Belgium, as individuals acted to shed the shackles of powerful state intuitions of surveillance, pedantry and threat.

In a 2018 article (yes, twenty years later) Adam Beckett of *The Guardian* commented on the book (the subject of the article was actually Jacob Rees-Mogg, Tory politician and son of William Rees-Mogg, who co-wrote the book).

He wrote:

For 380 breathless pages, Lord Rees-Mogg and a co-author, James Dale Davidson, an American investment guru and conservative propagandist, predicted that digital technology would make the world hugely more competitive, unequal and unstable. Societies would splinter. Taxes would be evaded. Government would gradually wither away. 'By

2010 or thereabouts,' they wrote, welfare states 'will simply become unfinanceable'. In such a harsh world, only the most talented, self-reliant, technologically adept person – 'the sovereign individual' – would thrive.

Yes, well. It turns out that differences of opinion about this book are, er, robust. But in some ways it was certainly prescient, in principle if not in detail, including this:

> Soon, you will pay for almost any transaction over the Net the same time you place it, using cybercash. This new digital form of money is destined to play a pivotal role in cybercommerce. It will consist of encrypted sequences of multihundred-digit prime numbers. Unique, anonymous, and verifiable, this money will accommodate the largest transactions. It will also be divisible into the tiniest fraction of value. It will be tradable at a keystroke in a multi-trillion-dollar wholesale market without borders.

Basically Bitcoin, twelve years before Satoshi's whitepaper. Not bad for a prediction, notwithstanding that researchers had quietly been tinkering with digital money for a couple of decades before publication.

As the late 2010s came into view, the book experienced somewhat of a revival. Ideological polarization, political instability, virulent nationalism and increasing income inequality had become worrying realities, and the book seemed to be worth another read, given that it spooled out a version of current troubles. A number of influencers did exactly that, ranging from PayPal CEO Peter Thiel to uber-venture capitalist Marc Andreessen. They all heaped praise on it, expressing as it did a libertarian view popular among many technology entrepreneurs.

Not everyone was similarly seduced, though. Critic E. Glen Weyl summarized it thus:

...it derives a series of 'predictions' about the collapse of most existing forms of social coordination/cooperation/control (nation states, corporations, unions etc.) into extreme anarcho-capitalism in which adherence to the rules of the game are enforced by various private entities, ranging from robots to mafias.[11]

He went to surgically eviscerate the book at some length. His review was entitled 'Sovereign Nonsense'.

Of course, like retrospectives of many past books about the near future, we will find some things that were wrong and some that were right, and we often overlook the former in favour of our worldview. The *Sovereign Individual* may have pushed its predicitions beyond modesty when it came to specifics and chronologies, but here is where it intersects with our story:

There are about 2.3 billion people living in electoral democracies (according to the website The Visual Capitalist).[12] While this is a minority of the world's population, they punch well above their weight in wealth, invention and influence. If we are lucky enough to be in this group, we have seen our options for thought and choice expand dramatically in the last fifty years, mainly through the basic protections of democratic rights (like free speech) and, in parallel, the many technologies that have expanded our horizons. Like knowledge acquisition, educational choices, employment modalities, communications, mobility and e-commerce.

Someone in the 1960s in the US may have had similar rights available to them, but options were more constrained because many of the technologies that we now enjoy were as yet undeveloped or even uninvented. So people could expect one or two jobs in a lifetime, a few TV channels, a local newspaper or two, rare long-distance travel, limited cuisine, a modest selection of local stores, hand-written letters from a distant friend and so on. The shelf of life choices is much fuller now than it was then.

And if you were over 'there', in a country in which the individual received less respect from the nation state, life was bare and monotonous, expansive dreams were not luxuries many people could afford and upward mobility was not a realistic expectation. This was most of the world fifty years ago.

As technology opened up our vistas in the last few decades, two things seem to have happened. In 'open' societies the individual has become more aspirational, vocal and even demanding about their wants and needs. Choices have created their own energy, although some would argue, in some cases, not always in the interests of community. And if you lived or live under an autocracy, the expansion of global communications like the Internet has at least presented brief glimpses of worlds that you might not ever have seen or even imagined fifty years ago.

There are still countries today who prefer their citizens to be blinkered in order to avoid challenges to groupthink, like China and North Korea and Saudi Arabia. Internet firewalls and telecommunications surveillance and other screws of censorship. But even then, tantalizing visions of a larger life filters though (OK, perhaps not in North Korea). A smorgasbord of choices, out of reach, but presumably not out of mind.

So our narrative flows along this path – technology progress has vastly expanded the universe of options in two different ways – both providing a near-endless menu of choices and (for some) the means to act on that choice.

See. Choose. Acquire. Own.

Own.

There are a host of criticisms lying in wait here, which I am sure that Eula Biss from Chapter 1 would be happy to level: there is too much to buy, the obsession and endless desire for acquisition and possession is certainly questionable. Yes to all of that, but there is an underlying nuance which I believe overrides this criticism.

It is that this rich trove of options allows individuals to express more fully who they are. Choice is the DNA of individualism. Whether we act on it this way or that way or even not at all, it creates the means for us to paint ourselves in colours that suit us, and more importantly, to repaint ourselves again anytime, and at our discretion. And so the aspirant sovereign individual emerges out of the constraints of the past – the consequences of widened options and the sloughing off of unwanted external guidance, demand and diktat.

(As I write this, I am bemused at how shockingly libertarian this sounds – I am actually not one of those – I sit comfortably at the centre of the libertarian-nanny state divide).

A short digression is necessary here, into the world of the 'sovereign citizen' as opposed to the 'sovereign individual'. These people, the so-called sovereign citizens (as opposed to individuals), are a different breed entirely. They are a motley and possibly dangerous smattering of groups who emerged in the US in the early 1970s and now have copycat movements worldwide. Their main claim is that they are not citizens of the state, that the state is illegitimate and has no right to mandate laws, and that they are free people, and swear no allegiance, except to God, who looms rather large in these groups.

The sovereign citizens movement is awash with groups bearing names like Christian Patriots, with made-up 'passports' and wacko interpretations of laws, harassment of law enforcement (clogging up courts) and avoidance of tax obligations. They should not be confused with the law-abiding human aspiring to have more sovereignty; seeking as much unfettered self-control over their lives, bodies and possessions as possible. In other words, an aspiration to self-ownership and reasonable independence from the state.

The sovereign individual, at least as painted by Davidson and Rees-Mogg, attracts a fair bit of derision. As John Donne famously reminded us, 'No man is an island, entire of itself; every man is a piece of the continent.' It is selfish, crass, even brutish, this tendency to be self-owned. Stop being a damn narcissist! Join the team! Yes well, this divide between individualism and collectivism sits at the centre of much more informed debates than I might muster, but it does not matter where one sits on this spectrum; it is also true that even the most civic-minded and team-spirited of us still seeks the means to self-define. It may not be a Prada bag that we want. It may be a book, a degree, a song. Ownership, especially now in this age, does not require wealth. Its riches are its diversity, not its cost.

In any event, like all other migrations of power, the technologically-fuelled catalyst for individual sovereignty is seeing pushback, even violence from those who seek to maintain power and control. Bob Simon, in an article for *Bitcoin Magazine* in 2021 put it succinctly:

> Sovereignty … is a zero-sum game. When individuals gain sovereignty, the state necessarily loses sovereignty over them. As citizens continue to take advantage of new technological innovations, institutions will naturally struggle to reclaim power.

OK. So a couple of guys write a book mainly about social disruption and the emergence of extreme individualism, powered largely by new applied technologies. The book gets new life, as social disruption does indeed start bubbling up in disturbing ways, perhaps partially tied to the authors' thesis, and partially because of other factors.

What does this have to do with the blockchain? Plenty, because the blockchain has become a Trojan horse that provides a surprising means of achieving the sovereignty that was previously out of reach. As we have discussed earlier, the blockchain has enabled ownership in ways not only previously unthinkable (dynamic, flexible, infinitely definable in its incarnations), but perhaps more importantly, ownership of things which previously had no easy path to ownership at all, like our behaviour patterns on the Web or opinions expressed on social media. The arrival of a new set of tools that will enable us to prove ownership of, well, anything material, digital or even corporeal expands our access to sovereignty, whether we care or not.

Which brings me to David Chaum.

One of the matters that has been less prominent in the discussion in the *Sovereign Individual* and the more general subject of individualism has been the matter of privacy. The underlying theme of this book concerns the blockchain's impact on ownership, and how the mathematics of secret-keeping has enabled that.

Privacy and ownership are close cousins. You may own an expensive NFT and choose to do it publicly. But if you have a secret that you do not wish to share, then we are in the territory of privacy, which is really just another form of ownership. And I am not talking here about simply your password. Any secret – which charity you contributed to, which websites you chose to visit, who you choose to call, when you choose to call them.

As much as we are defined by what we own publicly, we are similarly defined by what we keep secret and own privately.

David Chaum received his PhD at Berkeley at a time when cryptography was in full blossom in the early 1980s. In an interview with him that I listened to on a podcast called *Bankless*,[13] he talked about having been obsessed with secrets from an early age (one does casually wonder why), and how this naturally led him into cryptography, the science of secrets. Which brought him in close contact with some of the early crypto luminaries already discussed in this book – Diffie, Hellman, Merkle. And others who went on to their big achievements – Bill Joy who started Sun Microsystems (where the programming language Java was nurtured, as was an early version of the operating system Unix) and Eric Schmidt who went on to run Google from 2001 to 2010.

David Chaum has become somewhat of an icon in the last ten years within the crypto community, largely because of his 1982 dissertation, where he essentially described the technology of the blockchain. It was mysteriously titled 'Computer Systems Established, Maintained, and Trusted by Mutually Suspicious

Groups'.[14] And then a later paper titled 'Blind Signatures for Untraceable Payments',[15] which described another core piece of the modern blockchain: digital signatures. His icon status has been further burnished, I assume, because everyone seems to love him: he is smiling, talkative and generous with his knowledge, looking every bit the portly bearded uncle who is always laden with gifts and laughter when he comes over to visit.

There are many more quivers to Chaum's bow; his research output is a marvel – so many major innovations in the field have his imprimatur on them. Which has of course left a lot of people making a credible case that he is in fact Satoshi Nakamoto, which he does not confirm or deny. But let's not go there.

He has an important case to make about the centrality of privacy to blockchain and its spawn, and to the general lack of understanding of the difference between what we think is private ('oh, it's cool, it's encrypted') and real privacy. This is an obsession of his; he constantly hammers this home in his blog and public appearances.

Privacy does not only relate to something being hidden and accessible to only an authorized party. Like a Telegram or WhatsApp message, which indeed encrypts your message, the actual content. He is rather energetic about the fact that it is as important to also hide the 'metadata' – like who sent the message, who it was sent to, when it was sent. This metadata is easily available to third parties who eavesdrop; no great skill is required.

And, as we will see in the next chapter, 'privacy' and 'anonymity' are often confused – they achieve two different things.

Chaum, in support of his 'shred the metadata' clarion call, tells a fascinating story about the CIA-backed overthrow of the democratically elected president of Chile in 1970, Salvador

Allende. It turns out that one of the most important tools that they had at their disposal was 'trafficking data', which was a daily report of who called who and at what time in their 1970s style telephone network, thus allowing them to piece people and events together in space and time. They couldn't get the actual conversations, but the 'metadata' was enough for them to help overthrow a foreign government. (This is all in the public record now, acknowledged by the CIA in 2000.)

Chaum has written extensively on the metadata vulnerability in modern messaging systems, disingenuously obfuscated with the words like 'end-to-end encryption', which seem to satisfy most of us. Yes, our data may be encrypted, but our metadata isn't, and that is a treasure trove of information for anyone seeking to find out about you without you knowing.

It turns out that Chaum has solved this and other problems and has numerous products and initiatives just now stepping out into the sunshine, all bundled into the xx network, the decentralized platform he founded, including a quantum-resistant high-speed blockchain with integrated cryptographic payments and metadata 'shredded' messaging. All based on immutable ownership (Chaum prefers the word 'control') and privacy. It is making waves in the deep technosphere, with whispers of 'this is actually the real Web 3' beginning to circulate.

The tagline in the middle of the xx network home website page says:

BUILDING A WORLD WHERE YOUR LIFE BELONGS TO YOU.

Yup, that about says it all.

* * *

Before we leave this topic, a word about culture. One of our core propositions in this book is that new technologies, including (and especially) blockchain, have increased our opportunities for individualism. It turns out that this striving for self-ownership is strongly tied to specific cultures, and not all of them have an equal urgency to achieve it.

Geert Hofstede, who died in 2020 was Professor Emeritus at the University of Maastricht in The Netherlands. He is one of the most widely cited European social scientists, having developed a framework for measuring global cultural differences. These are – Individualism, Power Distance, Uncertainty Avoidance, Masculinity, Long-Term Orientation, and Indulgence vs. Restraint.

In August 2022, the podcast *Freakonomics* did a series on what makes Americans different. They spoke to Geert Hofstede's son, also a social scientist academic, and who worked on these cultural matters with his father. The podcast goes through each of these cultural dimensions, but lingers for a while on individualism and where it is most prevalent among cultures. Both Geert and Gert Jan have done large cross-cultural studies on these traits, and guess who comes out on top of the individualism rating?

The US.

No surprise there: it is where most of the cryptographic innovations were developed (along with the UK), and where most of the intellectual energy around crypto and its impact is centred.

So a caveat. The future of blockchain and its influence on ownership will not be equally distributed around the world. It will grow its deepest roots in the most individualistic of cultures, which as we have already mentioned, are largely found in electoral democracies.

Chapter 5

THE FOG OF PRIVACY AND
THE FEAR OF ANONYMITY

Privacy – and its centrality to human aspiration – has spawned a vibrant activist industry, with non-profit organizations dedicated to the protection of privacy dotting the landscape in surprising numbers. There is the famed Electronic Frontier Foundation (EFF), formed just before the Internet age, catalysed by an FBI visit to the home of a techie named John Perry Barlow, accusing him of stealing source code for some Macintosh internal chips. He realized quickly that the FBI had no understanding of code and technology at all, and that as personal computers and their progenies continued their spread into our lives, opportunities for the state to infringe on constitutional rights would be rife. With others he formed EFF to provide assistance to people whose digital lives were being malevolently intruded, which then attracted funding from a slew of technology influencers, including Steve Wozniak, Mitch Kapor and Stuart Brand.

And so we have the Electronic Privacy Information Center, the Tor Project, the Freedom of the Press Foundation, noyb.eu ('none of your business'), the Centre for Democracy and Technology, the Electronic Privacy Information Center, to name just a few. Privacy is a big deal, worth protecting, worth lobbying for, worth funding.

So when did privacy start to be seen as a human right? An article from Privacy Hub by Dana Vioreanu[16] gives us this:

In 1891, privacy was described for the first time as a human right. The American lawyers Samuel Warren and Louis Brandeis named it *'the right to be let alone'*.

The author rolls back further to a case in 1624 in Plymouth, the 1871 US Postal Act and the Fourth amendment to the US Constitution (wait, we'll get there). And in other countries, similar clamouring from populations who felt as though they could be heard. She mentions earlier events. Like prohibitions against unauthorized reading of people's correspondence in fourteenth century Europe.

We introduced David Chaum and his cryptographic expressions of privacy and anonymity in the previous chapter. The matter of privacy as a human right is a wide and contested subject spilling noisily into the pot of culture and politics. Particularly where it colours our understanding of ownership.

Everyone who doesn't have their head in the sand knows that in 2022 the Supreme Court of the United States overturned Roe v Wade (it was on 22nd June). The court didn't ban pregnancy termination. They said that this was not the Supreme Court's business, it should never have been their business, let the states decide. Without wishing to delve into the molten hot arguments that ensued and continue across the angry divides of American opinion, there is a related matter that many people do not know.

It was this. The original 22nd January 1973 case, which resulted in the protection of a woman's right to choose abortion, was argued on the basis of *privacy*. A woman's body is owned by her alone, and what she chooses to do with it, it was argued, was a private matter. It essentially armoured and encased the matter of bodily ownership within a right to privacy. Even the great Justice Ruth Bader Ginsberg was concerned that this argument was flimsy, and stated that she would have preferred an argument based on equal protection, which would have been far stronger.

In any event, privacy as an argument for abortion rights is obviously an extreme example (at least in its societal impact), but this underlines its importance in our understanding of ownership. Moreover, the issue of privacy itself is a cultural determinant. There are cultures like the US in which privacy is a cherished right, perhaps not broadly and directly encoded into the original Constitution, but something everyone knows and feels as an expression of America's general views of freedom. There are actually six amendments which imply privacy, like religious choice or the sanctity of the home, but it is not a fundamental right, like freedom of assembly or the right to petition.

Move over to other countries and you will find cultures for whom the Western world's expectation of privacy is nothing short of shocking. As a political tool, we read about this every day. For instance, China's mass surveillance of citizens is in the process of being intensified by orders of magnitude by their eYuan, which is a state-sponsored cryptocurrency in which every single instance of spend by a citizen can be tracked and stored and analysed. It is a complete disassembling of financial privacy and anonymity. It is even more striking for the fact that many Chinese citizens (most perhaps – polls are not easy to come by in that country) have little issue with that – there is not as much cultural expectation of privacy as there is in liberal democracies.

The same obviously holds true in deeply religious societies, where the whole notion of privacy is weakened when it is obvious that God sees all. Even Catholicism and its confessional makes the revelation of sinful personal secrets part of the requirements of redemption.

Notwithstanding all of these differing interpretations, the right is actually codified in the United Nations Declaration of Human Rights, article 12:

> No one shall be subjected to arbitrary interference with his privacy, family, home or correspondence, nor to attacks upon his honour and reputation. Everyone has the right to the protection of the law against such interference or attacks.

One should arch an eyebrow when considering that North Korea, China and others signed their names against this. There are also others that give privacy its due like the European Convention on Human Rights and the Swiss Federal Constitution.

And of course, the Fourth Amendment to the US Constitution:

> The right of the people to be secure in their persons, houses, papers, and effects, against unreasonable searches and seizures, shall not be violated, and no warrants shall issue, but upon probable cause, supported by oath or affirmation, and particularly describing the place to be searched, and the persons or things to be seized.

'To be secure… against unreasonable seizures'. Reads like a billboard for cryptographically secured ownership, doesn't it?

* * *

But anonymity does not fare as well.

Anonymity and privacy are different. Close cousins, sometimes, but not always. Anonymity refers only to keeping your identity private, but not necessarily your actions (like using a pseudonym or handle to post something). Privacy means keeping some things to yourself, including your actions, if you so choose, and which may or may not include anonymity.

Which throws a curveball our way. Yeah, privacy, we can all buy into some version of that, it is intuitively acceptable to everyone. But anonymity is far more complex, and immediately raises the spectre of mal-intent. The only people who want to do stuff anonymously are the people who have something to hide – a trope we have all heard many times, and likely fall prey to occasionally.

Which, of course, is not true at all.

(There was a hilarious plot in a *Curb Your Enthusiasm* episode in which the Larry David character makes a named donation to the new wing of a children's hospital, while his best friend Ted Danson makes an anonymous donation. His friend then 'leaks' that he is behind the anonymous donation and gets all of the adulation, much to Larry's distress. A funny twist on real-life leaky anonymity).

But in truth, reasons for why we, as individuals, may seek anonymity are myriad and circumstances are varied. Like making your mark on a voting ballot. Anonymity is what we seek, but not privacy. We want our vote heard.

Anonymity sits at the heart of blockchains like Bitcoin and Ethereum. In all of the major blockchains, the actual transactions are not private at all: they are public, by design. It is only the real-world identities of senders and receivers which are anonymous.

This has made regulators and other surveillers blind and grumpy. Until 8th August 2022, when a bomb exploded right in the middle of the cryptosphere, the impact of which is still being felt, its implications not yet clear.

There is a corner of the US Treasury called the OFAC – the Office of Foreign Assets Control. It monitors global bad behaviour and mandates sanctions when appropriate. Big serious sanctions. What kind of bad behaviour? Terrorists, money launderers, tax criminals, narcotics traffickers, anti-US military belligerents. Countries, institutions, companies, individuals. Anyone who is deemed to be a threat to national security in any way.

You do not want to be on this list, because it is almost impossible to get off, unless of course you repent and mend your ways and become an ally, which rarely happens in real life. And even if you do, well, you may never get off, because the US Treasury has a long memory.

If you go to their website page at home.treasury.gov you will find lists of embargoed people and countries and organizations. For instance, you will find a list of 'SDNs'. Those are the 'Specially Designated Nationals'. People. It is nearly 2,000 pages long. Tightly packed with names, tens of thousands of them in multiple columns, who will never be visiting the Grand Canyon. Then there is a whole slew of other lists, with other sanctioned entities like states. And these lists end up all over the place – visa offices, entry points to the US, CIA,

FBI, the police, in the databases of intelligence agencies of US allies, in the supercomputers of the NSA.

This is not where it ends, because the law says that even if you are a decent, law-abiding citizen and you unwittingly do business with any of these entities, you are breaking the law. If a company is sanctioned for making military widgets you don't dare buy toothbrushes from its other consumer health subsidiary. How much would you be breaking the law if you did that? Well, many Americans have gone to jail since OFAC was established in 1950.

In short, you want to spend your life well clear of OFAC and its long arms and long lists. It's only trouble for the people on their lists, and trouble for people who know people on its lists and trouble for people who even vaguely brush against people on its lists.

So what happened on 22nd August?

OFAC sanctioned not a person, not a country, not a legal entity *but a piece of computer code.* They listed the address on the Ethereum blockchain where the code resided. This was unprecedented; all other OFAC lists are tied to persons.

Specifically, that code was a crypto project called Tornado Cash. It was what is called a mixer in crypto speak. It allows anyone to send cryptocurrency to Tornado Cash, where they mix it up with lots of other people's cryptocurrencies, so that it can be sent on, without anyone (like a government) being able to track where it originated. In short, it guarantees anonymity of not only human identities, but also of the metadata; its original sending address is shredded. Meaning an injection of truly deep anonymity into financial transactions.

It has no corporation or partnership or person that runs it that can be sued or sanctioned or imprisoned. It runs autonomously, without a head. It is, as they say, autonomous, decentralized. And anyone who used Tornado Cash after 22nd August 2022 was suddenly breaking a big scary federal law and could go to jail.

Why did OFAC do this? It is because many, many cyber-criminals use Tornado Cash to cover their tracks. Including an estimated $1.5 billion stolen by North Korea in various cybercrimes (there are indications it could be much more). But here is the important bit – there are many, many regular people who simply use Tornado Cash because they want a particular transaction to be entirely anonymous.

A perfect example here is the co-founder of Ethereum, the second-largest blockchain. Vitalek Buterin stated a few days after the embargo that he had previously used Tornado Cash to donate to charities, which he did not want made public.

The now-sanctioned technology behind Tornado Cash is entirely neutral – it is used by both bad actors and good actors.

Under the OFAC sanctions it immediately became illegal to send money to or from a Tornado Cash wallet. Given that hundreds of millions of dollars were affected in one way or another, you can imagine the chaos that ensued, with thousands of people unable to access their currency for fear of imprisonment, and hundreds of important crypto projects slamming on all sorts of brakes.

And then it got even more Kafkaesque, as some anonymous crypto holders (possibly outside of the US, but who knows) started sending tiny amounts of cryptocurrency through Tornado Cash to famous celebrities in the US, such as Dave Chappelle, Logan Thomas and Jimmy Fallon, thereby directly incriminating them in terms of the law and making a complete mockery of the whole OFAC exercise. It has been referred to as 'taintgate' – the celebrities are all now tainted and possibly under investigation by the US government.

Is Tornado Cash a destination for crypto-laundering? Yes. Is it also a destination for utterly legitimate use for people seeking transaction privacy? Yes. Tornado Cash is NEUTRAL. It is a piece of code. It is like sanctioning cars because they are always used in getaways.

Tornado Cash will be replaced in a second; mixers are not complicated to design and code. Any number of others are already operating in the open, including one integrated into David Chaum's xx network

Will it survive courts? OFAC is already under legal challenge, both on the legal principle and on behalf of innocent citizens who lost money. It seems to me that a piece of code run, operated and owned by *no one* is not criminal and cannot be tethered to malign intent, but we live in a fast-changing world, and I am neither a legislator or jurist, so I may be entirely wrong.

But I will rest my amateur opinion in this, which can be found in OFAC documentation:

> The ultimate goal of sanctions is not to punish, but to bring about a positive change in behavior. Each year, OFAC removes hundreds of individuals and entities from the SDN List. Each removal is based on a thorough review by OFAC.

I can see the killer blow in the final episode of the TV show now: 'You honour, if this is the ultimate goal of sanctions, how then does the prosecution propose to get an immutable piece of code to change its behaviour?'

* * *

So then, anonymity, privacy and, of course, security. Ownership seeks the support of each of these in different circumstances. We might wish to own something anonymously, or publicly. We might wish the details of the ownership to be private, while the fact of the ownership be public (I own a Picasso, but I'm not telling you which one!). We will, presumably, always want security, to have our ownership resistant to seizure, to have the control to cede or sell to be ours, and ours alone.

Lots of mixing and matching there. All of it is now given life by the mathematical wizardry of cryptographers like David Chaum and Satoshi and his descendants.

I close with a last observation about anonymity. This is the centre of the war between individual and state, in some fundamental and profound way. States abhor anonymity, even if they are minimally tolerant of privacy and energetically supportive of security. States need control. This is not a criticism; without control it cannot guide an economy and policy. It is hard to control anonymity; that is why, at the very least, we start with a birth certificate and a social security card (in the US) and then passport and then all of the other codifications of non-anonymity.

Without them the state and the individual lose what binds them to common purpose.

Chapter 6

ETHEREUM, THE SMART CONTRACT AND THE FORK IN THE ROAD

English mathematician Alan Turing, who tragically committed suicide in June 1954, was largely unknown outside a reverent band of mathematicians and computer scientists and students until 2014 arrived and a movie called *The Imitation Game* was made, starring Benedict Cumberbatch. It made Alan Turing a household name. I was an undergraduate at university when I first came upon the 'Turing Machine', a thought experiment dreamed up by Alan Turing that reduced a computer to its simplest operating functions, whose rules of operation served not only as a philosophical basis for computer science, but for proximal studies like artificial intelligence.

His tragic and glorious genius has been widely covered now, and almost everyone has glancing recognition of his genius in many areas from cryptanalysis to philosophy.

Except that we need to talk about the phrase 'Turing complete'.

We have already mentioned Vitalek Buterin and the Ethereum blockchain, which he conceived and developed, along with other colleagues and contributors. He was, and remains, its main guru. The whitepaper by Satoshi had described the design principles of the Bitcoin blockchain (the word 'blockchain' was actually never mentioned in the paper). The blockchain was duly developed and its one and only *raison d'être* was the peer-to-peer sending or receiving of a token, also called Bitcoin, which soon attracted real commercial value and today commands the attention of public zeitgeist when thinking about crypto.

The Bitcoin blockchain was designed to do this one single thing well – act as a secure harness, database and transport system for the Bitcoin cryptotoken (cryptocurrency if you like, now that it has a value that can be used for payment). This was by design; it was never envisaged to be a Swiss Army knife, even though some weak tools were provided to expand its functionality slightly.

Vitalek was very taken with Bitcoin, even started a magazine called *Bitcoin Magazine*, an early entrant into the now massive crypto media space. He hung out with Bitcoin nerds, enthusiasts and developers at early meet-ups and conferences.

But at some point, one imagines, he said to himself:

'Wait! Why is all of this magic packed into the blockchain constrained to this one thing? I mean, the Bitcoin blockchain is very cool and all, but the technological plumbing sitting underneath is underutilized. If I develop a programming language that gives full access to the wonders of the blockchain, who knows what people might invent? There must be more to blockchains than just Bitcoin.'

Perhaps his thinking didn't look anything like this at all, but this phrase, 'develop a programming language', certainly sat at the centre of his idea.

And he did develop it. And it changed everything.

So let's go a little deeper. In the bowels of the theoretical world of computer science languages there is the concept of a 'Turing complete' machine. Here is a definition I picked up from one of many on the web:

> A Turing Complete machine refers to a machine that, given enough time and memory along with the necessary instructions, can solve any computational problem, no matter how complex.

The definition introduces some things that we needed to exclude for the sake of simplicity (like 'machine' and 'memory'). So how about this: 'A Turing complete language can theoretically compute any problem imaginable, as long as it is computable'?

Why is this important? Because there are other computer languages that can only solve a constrained set of problems, for instance, the 'weak' scripting language available on the Bitcoin blockchain, which was only ever meant to do a finite number of things. And Vitalek believed that it was simply not possible for anyone to know what some teenager may dream up in a garage when given full access to the armoury of the blockchain.

So Vitalek and his team spun up a blockchain that looked a lot like the Bitcoin blockchain, and added a programming language that would allow for, well, any idea to be coded, tested and perhaps to flourish. A Turing complete programming language, essentially unbounded in its possibilities.

The Ethereum whitepaper[17] describing this was released in 2013, and the first version of the Ethereum blockchain was released in 2015 to great excitement among the then small crypto community. It has its own Bitcoin-like currency called 'ether' or ETH, pronounced 'eeth'. And it was let loose on the world, downloadable by anyone.

This whitepaper is a little more complex and technical than the Bitcoin whitepaper. But most computer science students, even undergraduates, can fully understand the programming snippets included in it, and even those without any technical background can get the important principles. The prose is precise, the structure clear, the arguments and rationale well grounded. While reading it my first thoughts were how professional and mature the document was.

Vitalek was a teenager when he wrote it.

There are a number of other things in this document that bear comment. The way the document flows is to talk first about the Bitcoin blockchain, its capabilities and weaknesses, and then to describe how Ethereum's core proposition, integrating a Turing complete programming language, solves all of those weaknesses (the 'programs' are referred to as 'smart contracts'). Parts of the paper's value is that it goes further than this. It doesn't simply say 'we have a programming language and therefore we can do more, so go and build something'. It not only describes precisely how some of the Bitcoin weaknesses could be addressed but then goes on to suggest a slew of possible future projects that could be implemented.

Here are some of the ideas he floated – stablecoins, financial derivatives, identity and reputation systems, decentralized file storage, marketplace exchanges, gambling, prediction markets, crop insurance, multi-signature authorizations, decentralized autonomous organizations. He didn't just reel off a list, as I have done, he also described important implementation details. Perhaps I am overstating the case here, but this seems prescient to the point of soothsaying.

In essence, Vitalek was describing the future. He was not 100% accurate, of course: a few of them did not materialize, at least in the form that he described in the paper. And he completely missed a few, notably NFTs, which he has admitted in recent years that he never saw coming.

In any event, Vitalek and his colleagues sat down and waited to see what would be invented. Actually, no – that's not strictly true. Because he had firm and fully formed ideas of cool stuff that might be built, he continued to write long articulate blogs which expanded on his short list in the paper, describing more deeply why and how these applications should be built. A number of the biggest and most valuable crypto projects in the world started this way, including Uniswap, developed by mechanical engineer Hayden Adams, who read a blog by Vitalek, and thought, hmm. Hayden did not really know how to program computers. He learned. And Uniswap, a crypto exchange he built, now handles as much volume as some of the largest exchanges in the world after just a few years in existence.

The native Ethereum cryptocurrency ETH grew very quickly in value, and so the Ethereum Foundation was formed, which helped with the financing of projects. Some suggested by Vitalek. And also by members of his team. And colleagues. And then outsiders and tinkerers and dreamers and hobbyists and builders and professionals. It was basically crypto-homesteading writ large. A wide-open sun-kissed land, stretching from horizon to horizon, just waiting for people to stake their claims to decentralization.

And so what of ownership? The paper mentions ownership numerous times, but this one sentence provides the fountain from which our entire proposition drinks:

'Ethereum... is essentially the ultimate abstract foundational layer: a blockchain with a built-in Turing-complete programming language, allowing anyone to write smart contracts and decentralized applications where they can create their own arbitrary rules for ownership...'

Which brings us to the fork in the road, part of this chapter's title.

From 2010 to 2015 there was really only one big road. Cryptocurrencies. First Bitcoin and then competitors and copycats. We will talk about cryptocurrencies in more detail in an upcoming chapter, but these were and are, essentially single-use blockchains. A way to transfer value from one address to another, under the benign but unwavering gaze of mathematical certainty, without interference or assistance or undue surveillance. With the arrival of Ethereum (and its subsequent competitors and copycats) the road forked.

In one direction: single-function blockchains, like Bitcoin. Which facilitates the user's irrevocable and secure ownership of the token that represents that single use. In most cases, this is the ability to own and transfer money.

In the other direction endless apps (or dapps, decentralized apps), encoded in programs called smart contracts. Allowing users the ability to own financial products and derivatives and digital files and voting rights and all manner of things yet to be imagined. It is a very colourful, essentially infinite landscape of ownership possibilities that has been enabled by Ethereum's Turing-complete programming language acting as Ethereum's external interface to ideas.

There may well be other forks in the road, but it is unlikely. I am reminded of a cute graphic animation that I once saw. A desk covered with stuff. Books and a rotary telephone and a clock and a radio and a TV and a paper diary and some games. About twenty or thirty single-function objects we might have reached out to in our daily lives, circa 1970. The animation shows the arrival of the smartphone and each one of these objects floats up off the desk and into the phone. Not all that original, but nicely rendered. The manufacturer of the phone might change, as may the prevailing best programmable blockchain at some time in the future, but it will still be Turing-complete and be able to do just about anything and provide for infinite opportunities to define and secure different types of ownership, because there are infinite ways to design and write a program.

And single-function programmable blockchains, like Bitcoin? They have the advantage of being unencumbered by trying to be too many things to too many people, optimized to perform their primary, tightly defined, task with excellence and precision. And secondary layers can still be built on top of it, like the Lightning Network, which has enabled exponentially faster payments than the core Bitcoin blockchain, by allowing two parties who pre-establish trust with each other. There is still long life in the single-function blockchain, just as there is use in single-function, highly customized real-world machines.

We will discuss cryptocurrencies later, but redefinition of ownership discussed in this book has been largely driven by the marriage of the Turing-complete language and the blockchain, which expanded this world from mathematical secured-ownership of money to, well, ownership of anything that can be titled, tethered and cryptographically secured.

Chapter 7

SEE YOU IN COURT

A somewhat embarrassing tale.

I am reasonably experienced in this world, having invested and traded modestly in this and that since 2017. But I have also found myself on the wrong side of optimism and experience more than once. The nastiest of these was getting caught out with some of my cryptocurrency in the custody of a small exchange that went bust, either through theft or software bugginess, most likely the former (the case is ongoing).

I had broken the most cardinal rule of crypto trading, which was to leave the custody of my private keys with the exchange. This was the embarrassing part: I had been warned for years, and knew well the little platitude 'not your keys, not your coins', and I understood the risks.

One day I opened the exchange webpage to check my account (which I rarely did), only to find a scary note on the front page of the website that informed me that the exchange had gone into liquidation. I will skip over a number of details here, but there is an important legal matter I want to probe.

A liquidator was duly appointed by the relevant authorities and a bunch of my fellow hapless investors, after a few false starts, finally found a rare attorney who understood crypto and exchanges and wallets and keys. Immediately a number of questions arose. Who owns the cryptocurrency that was on the blockchain? Was it the exchange or the investors? Were we creditors or was the exchange merely a third party custodian of our coins, which would put us ahead of simple creditors in the scramble to retrieve whatever was still there?

Worse, some of the investors had transferred money from their 'tradfi' banks to the exchange, who facilitated the purchase of the cryptocurrencies on their behalf, whereas others (including me), had transferred my cryptocurrency to this exchange from another crypto exchange, not from a bank. I had a record of the wallet-to-wallet transaction from Binance to the new exchange. There was an account management system at the exchange which had a record of all depositors names and transactions, but no one seemed to be able to get access to it.

The liquidator presumably had access to all this information, but was not forthcoming or simply couldn't be bothered. Remember that the liquidator would like as few claimants as possible; they get to keep a percentage of what is left. It is not in their interests to help.

What became evident very quickly is that the liquidator knew nothing of wallets, private keys, blockchain, addresses, and did not seem interested in finding out. Similarly, the ultimate governing authority of this matter is a state agency called The Master of the High Court. Crypto knowledge within this institution is similarly non-existent.

I don't know how this will all shake out (I am not optimistic I will ever see anything back), but there is a cautionary tale here, which is that this new technology has moved at a speed which has immediately outrun the network of legal and judicial and statutory expertise. There are some attorneys who have come up to speed, but judges and courts are far behind, and the pace of regulation and legislation is the slowest of lumbering state beasts.

The historical legal definitions of property ownership and property rights and the contestations that have been adjudicated in court have a long and colourful and often angered history; there are lawyers who specialize in its many incarnations and are deft at deeds, claims, transfer, titles and all the other arcana of ownership. But suddenly they are wrestling with something entirely new, something for which there is little regulation and even less case precedent.

Consider the complications that have arisen in law. You buy an NFT tethered to a piece of art; the record of purchase and ownership of which will be immutability lodged on the blockchain, secured by your private key. Let us, for simplicity, say that the art is a digital photograph taken by a famous photographer, with her digital SLR camera. The NFT is minted by the photographer and it is listed on an NFT market, where you make your purchase.

Here are the potential stumbling blocks on the legal view of this: not all countries have a legal definition of NFTs, which is the first problem. In the UK, at least, in an important ruling on 10th June 2022 (Bankers Trust vs Ozone Network Inc),[18] the judge, in granting an injunction against the defendant said, 'There is clearly going to be an issue at some stage as to whether non-fungible tokens constitute property for the purposes of the law of England and Wales, but I am satisfied… that there is a least a realistically arguable case that such tokens are to be treated as property as a matter of English law.'

OK, property then, at least by this decision, which helps. But what do you own? You own the NFT, although not necessarily the photograph. The NFT is a receipt for the photograph. Are you sure you own unique rights to view, or do you own the intellectual property itself (most buyers are not getting intellectual property rights, even though they think they are)? Is this image one of many identical digital prints that the author is selling? These are all matters that should be encoded in the smart contract, but this may not be clear to the naive buyer.

What happens if someone accesses the photo and changes a single pixel, and relists with a new NFT, claiming it to be the original? Or even claims it to be something entirely new, with at least identical value, because, you know, it's just one pixel different? Was there a digital signature included of the original image encoded with the NFT which made yours the real deal? Or was it simply an URL pointing at a photo somewhere on a server. And if that server is destroyed or its IP address changed? What then do you own?

And what if your NFT is stolen from your wallet because of a bug in the wallet software, and you see 'your' photo appear somewhere else, under some new NFT ownership? To whom do you turn to have your photo returned, and how is that achieved? Is there a sheriff somewhere who can repo your NFT?

I chose NFTs for this example because they are a reasonably pure and well-known expression of blockchain ownership. But the crypto oceans are awash with other blockchain-owned creatures. A token representing a right to vote in a DAO governance scheme, for instance. What is this thing that is owned? If you own a right, can it be stolen if the token is stolen? It can be ceded or sold by you, but what if you unknowingly sell your right to vote to a bad actor. How would anyone know? And would you be liable?

There is a bewildering confusion of ownership threads that await clarity from the legislators and courts. But there is a crack of light appearing, particularly one which shone suddenly in the UK in August of 2022.

One of the most pressing matters of the entire crypto space started with the US Securities and Exchange Commission (SEC) growling at the initial coin offerings (ICOs) that grew like a cancer in the mid to late 2010s, and sanctioning some of them towards the end of that decade. Then other agencies started circling quickly, both in the US and elsewhere, mostly knee-jerking and walking stupidly into walls as they struggled (and continue to struggle) to understand this suite of new crypto assets. It was not surprising that everyone's first impulse was to take the square pegs of crypto and jam them into the round holes of hundred-year-old regulations.

It was hard to make them fit. Cryptotokens are shapeshifters, looking like currencies or shares or property or receipts or club memberships or governance votes depending on their underlying engines, where the tokens are 'emitted' by smart contracts for myriad different purposes. How in the world was regulation going to deal with these new things, the cryptotokens, whose shared name belies their diversity and flexibility?

* * *

The Law Commission of England and Wales was formed by an Act of Parliament in 1965, its mission to give advice to the government on various policy issues that Parliament may decide. And one of these issues, during 2022, was front and centre, with a report having been commissioned by the Ministry of Justice more than two years earlier. What are these strange things arising from the blockchain and other digital engines? How should they fit into our law?

The consultation paper dropped on 28th July 2022. It is titled in a typically understated British way – 'Digital Assets: Consultation Paper'.[19] It is not a recommendation for law and policy; its goal is to air the issues and invite comment, so that they can move one step closer to the additional gates and processes that end up in statutes. It is also 549 pages long, although there is a handy summary of twenty pages, mercifully provided by the Commission.

And it is a marvel of clear thinking about a new technology whose applications and impacts are barely understood, even by the cryptographers, mathematicians, computer scientists, economists and other builders who constructed its entangled and chaotic edifices.

The document is thick with the sort of commentary one would expect from policy professionals who had made sure to understand everything at some depth. This is evidenced in the appendices and references, which read like a set of reading requirements for several PhD theses. Their list of advisors is equally impressive, including the remarkable fact that the authors reference several tweets from leading members of the crypto community as support for their arguments. I was tickled by this, because it is indeed true that most of the deep thinking about crypto happens on social media, and much of it through tweetstorms and Twitter links.

I only want to zoom in on a few observations about the content of this document. The first is that the Commission recognizes the need for a new definition in property law. There have only ever been two types of property in English law – 'things in possession' and 'things in action' (the latter being a legal right, like a debt or right to sue on breach of contract). The authors have correctly determined that a digital asset is neither and have recommended the creation of the third type of property called a 'digital object'.

This is the core of the paper:

> Having suggested that the law should explicitly recognise a distinct third category of personal property, we describe the criteria that we consider a thing must exhibit before it properly can fall within that third category and thereby constitute a data object. We apply these criteria to different types of digital asset including digital files, domain names, email accounts, in-game digital assets, carbon credits and crypto-tokens.

The legal ramifications go deep and are carefully unpacked. How is a data object different from the other two types of properties? How does a data object differ from mere information? What are the ownership considerations? It is interesting that they discuss ownership and then ditch the word in favour of the word 'control', much in the same way as cryptographer David Chaum did in our coverage of him in a previous chapter.

The authors go even further: they spend a great deal of time on the definition and classification of cryptotokens and recognize, as we did earlier in this chapter, that this catch-all word is insufficient, nuances between the different types of tokens need to be clearly understood, implying a more fine-grained regulatory regime than many in government and in civil society might imagine.

My enthusiasm for this document and its authors is a little fanboy-ish. Never mind the long version, just the twenty-page summary made my heart beat faster and renewed my faith in institutions, which, like many people in the world right now, is somewhat battered. So before I get carried away, I leave you with one final comment.

The polarization of positions around the cryptoverse and its impending and stumbling arrival in our legal canon has brought out extreme positions (on all sides) that argue from the perspectives of alarm and hyperbole – from the feared jackboot of the state on one side to accusations of uncaring and dangerous libertarianism on the other. But as is evident from this document I submit that the laws will be debated and promulgated and perhaps reworked over time, informed by the best efforts of the cool heads that thought about crypto and committed these words to paper.

We will return to the broader topic of global regulation later, where there is a storm of activity, but if you are in the UK, and if I see you in court on a crypto matter perhaps we'll have good laws to protect us.

Chapter 8

GROUND ZERO –
OWNING YOURSELF

There is an odd irony in that the most personal of all owner-ships, ourselves, seems to have been a relative latecomer to blockchain and the techno-philosophers who are building its future. But suddenly there is a great deal of activity in finding an intersection between personal identity and the blockchain, and whether that intersection has any efficacy and advantage. I have used the phrase 'personal identity' for simplicity, but I am really referring to 'self-sovereign identity', a phrase generally used to indicate not only our identity in the abstract, but our ability to have control over how, when and why that identity is compiled and released.

We have talked much about title deed regimes in this book – those memorialized codifications that attest to ownership of something or other, usually under the gaze of some title 'authority' or third party. Like a traffic licensing entity or a city municipality that registers titles to houses. The title authority has a core set of functions, which is to be the ulti-mate verifier of an authenticity of title and, in some cases, the issuer and custodian.

I would like to think that an external authority cannot hold sway over my identity in the same way state transport bureaucracies may have sway over my car ownership, but that is not the case. They can, and have, and do. If one were to peel back the many layers of human identity documentation and verification, there is a single solitary legal document on which everything else builds, and it is the birth certificate (which is itself a descendant of the baptismal logs from 500 AD, which the Church use to police and prevent cousin marriages).

In most cases birth certificates are a routine matter. The birth registration is filled out in the hospital, and everything flows from there. In the US it is called The Standard Certificate of Live Birth; there are 58 questions to answer over two pages. Most often filled in with the help of hospital staff, who presumably do most of the heavy lifting, given that I expect the last thing a new mother wants to attend to is a statutory document.

This document then serves as the rootstock for all other branches of our legal identity. Social Security cards (in the US), ID books, passports, school registrations, credit cards, membership cards and so on. Need for authentication of one or other of these documents is pretty much a constant in our lives – airports, points of sale, traffic stops, banks, entry to one venue or another. And similarly constant are the continual attempts by bad guys to steal one or more of these documents, if even for a short enough time to commit a little fraud, but occasionally for a lifetime, as has happened in cases of birth certificate forgery.

With the arrival of the Internet, things got a little more frenetic. Some of our physical documents simply got replicated electronically, like credit cards (but not passports, yet). But many web interactions needed less than that; just a small piece of us would do. And so slivers of our identity were carved off and handed to many anonymous operators, some legit, others less so. Big trusted brands like Amazon or Netflix, but small, untrusted ones too, like that online travel business offering impossible deals that suddenly went out of business, occasionally with our funds and often with some personal data about us too.

We provided usernames and passwords, often the same ones we always used because they were easy to remember. We gave credit card details, re-entered multiple times across many websites. We gave out our home address. Our mobile numbers. And then when social media arrived en masse we really dug deep, handed over personal photographs and posts and friends and CVs and locations and interests and the routes to our journeys across the Internet.

Most everyone swore up and down that they would take care of our identities. They really respected our privacy, they said. Earnest policies were written, and we were sometimes forced to read them, or at least scroll through them, usually fast.

But they didn't take care of our identities, did they?

The little pieces of us were often sold without our permission or knowledge. Lax security moats saw our favourite username-password combinations stolen and sold on the dark web, as in the 147 million people and their details leaked in the Equifax hack in 2017. And the total cost of this and other breaches that year was $654 million, according to a 2018 report by ForgeRock. The unluckiest of us got directly violated by ransomware, sometimes paying extortionate amounts for the return of priceless personal data that we had carelessly stored locally on our hard drives and had not sent into the safety of the cloud.

I recently went onto both Facebook and Google to find out how much data they have on me, because they now provide handy tools to do so, a recent surrender to public outrage. I was shaken by the files that they sent, both in their size and diversity. Some stuff going back decades. Sold along the way to anyone and everyone offering the purchase fee. That data represents part of my identity.

Rounding out this litany of identity issues is the tragedy of the undocumented, the legally *unidentified*; those 1.2 billion people around the world born into circumstances in which birth certificates and other legal documentation of personhood was simply never acquired, or lost and never regained, guaranteeing a lifetime of exclusion from most of the trappings of citizenry.

Yes, things have changed a bit. We can now request that our data not be shared, but most people simply don't bother, because you have to opt out, and who has the time and energy for that? And all the while the battle between cybercriminals and cyber-defenders continues to rage, each one alternatively winning and losing territory, while the rest of us go about our business and try to remember to upgrade our operating systems and download patches as soon as we are told. We are provided with new armour – password managers, two-factor authentication, facial recognition on our iPhones. And yet cybercrime continues – the US-based Insurance Information Institute reports that in the US in 2021, 47% of citizens experienced some form of financial identity theft, and its cost to the economy was $56 billion.

Let's pause for a moment to reflect on this – all this paperwork, these plastic cards, password-protected digital snippets. Surely that is not us. Which brings up questions about the true nature of identity. Who are we? It is clearly not the paperwork that attests to us.

So I offer this.

I am because of my mother. My name. My father. Siblings. Relatives. School teachers. Friends. Colleagues. Where I am and have been in time and space. Things that I own. My experience. My memories. My aspirations. My talents. Deeds. Certifications. I am the sum total of every moment lived, which means I will not be tomorrow what I am today.

I am not a birth certificate and its progeny.

But neither of the preceding two paragraphs are of much help to us, at least in terms of finding a technological foundation for protecting and controlling self-sovereign identity.

* * *

There is a wonderful open science website called Frontiers. org. It publishes papers and allows free and open access, likely a reaction against paywalled academic research sites. In hacking my way through the thicket of literature on self-ownership, self-sovereign identity and digital identity (DID) this site magically appeared on in my Google Search with the following tag line, all glittery trumpet fanfare – 'Establishing Self Sovereign Identity with Blockchain'.

Rarely does research present itself so vividly, so I gleefully went fishing.

Eleven articles on the subject are downloadable from the page. All written by smart people from great universities and research institutes. Each one with multiple links and citations to a couple of hundred years' worth of research, opinion and debate about identity.

One paper was particularly illuminating. It is by Phillip J. Windley of Brigham Young University, and it is entitled 'Sovrin: An Identity Metasystem for Self-Sovereign Identity'.[20]

Sovrin is a non-profit company that was set up in 2017 to develop an architecture and network for facilitating a self-sovereign identity service on the blockchain. The project has struggled somewhat, not for competitive reasons, I suspect, but because the project of properly defining what is referred to as a *meta-identity* framework (meaning that it exists independent of underlying enabling technology) and then building it and then testing it and then getting, er, the whole world to start using it, is somewhat of a HAM, a big Hairy Audacious Monster. I sincerely hope that they thrive, but it is some of Windley's commentary that I want to share.

We have given a few examples about misuse of our online identities by external institutions who wish to monetize us. Why should we care that much?

Windley puts it succinctly towards the end of his paper:

We use identity in the physical world without thinking about it. And when we do, there are patterns that are so ingrained in our ways of interacting that we do not give them a second thought. If we are to move more and more of our lives to the digital realm while also preserving agency and autonomy, we must create a digital world that allows us to jump the trust gap we inevitably have with people, organisations, and things when our interaction is digital.

The *trust gap*. Indeed. That sits at the core of just about everything crypto is trying to fix.

Windley articulates numerous critical layers of the identity question. The most important of these is that we have multiple identities, depending on to whom they are being revealed. To put it more pointedly, our identities only show themselves in the context of a *relationship*. What you reveal of yourself to your best friend will not be the same as what you reveal to your child or the customs official or the online e-commerce site. It is a profound realization. My identity is not who I am. It is what I reveal, by choice or instinct or conditioning.

There is another side to our identity relationships as described by the author. We are continually building on our identities, the result of time passing and the things that arrive in its wake. A new degree, a new job, a new skill mastered, a new mobile number. These are conferred on us by external parties – a university or mobile operator, for instance. They are called 'attributes' of identification and they change over time. The external parties who provide these attributes are also in a relationship with us; we attended courses at their institutions and took the exam, or we got a new SIM card and pay the mobile operator monthly.

These are the relationship dynamics on which Sovrin is built.

We now take a careless leap from principles and abstractions and directly into the three architectural layers of Sovrin.

- The Relationship layer – these are Credential Issuers (like a university), Holders (you and me) and Verifiers (like an employer seeking to verify your degree before hiring you).
- The Messaging layer – system must facilitate the ability for the three parties to talk to each other. Like – Hey, Amazon, here's my college degree, please hire me.
- The 'Trustworthy Attribute Exchange via Verified Credentials' layer – meaning that a credential must be immutably proved authentic, unforgeable, the real McCoy.

Which means... drum roll please... cryptography and digital signatures and... the blockchain.

So here we have it. The philosophy of me-ness, to the components of self-sovereignty, to the formulation of the 'relationship' principle, to cryptographically secured attributes of identity, to its full expression on the blockchain.

A final piece of this architecture. Only Holders (us) decide what verified credentials they want in their wallet, and what credentials and personal information they wish to share to whom, depending on context and relationship. And so digital identity returns to its rightful owner, under lock and key, provably authentic and verifiable, under our sovereign control.

The question of whether and when this solution or something similar will gain the traction it needs to free us from the sheer unreliability, insecurity and redundancy of our current inarticulate attempts to identify ourselves online is still open. But there is this – remember Tim Berners-Lee, who invented the world wide web? He now heads W3C, the World Wide Web Consortium, which defines standards for the Web.

On 19th July 2022, W3C approved a standard called Digital Identifier (DID) v1.0. It looks very much like Sovrin. That's a big deal.

* * *

In May of 2022 a paper appeared on the Social Science Research Network (SSRN). It was written by E. Glen Weyl, Puja Ohlhaver and none other than Ethereum's Vitalik Buterin.

The paper was somewhat theatrically titled 'Decentralized Society: Finding Web3's Soul'.[21] The title is followed by a quote from Lao Tzu, who was the historical founder of Taoism. I am not sure I really understood the deeper relevance of the quote, but it certainly announced that the paper was not going to be about anything as grubby as money or finance. In fact, the opening sentence of the paper is pretty clear: 'Web3 today centers around expressing transferable, financialized assets, rather than encoding social relationships of trust.'

The paper goes on to explain itself as a reaction to the purely material drivers of crypto-ownership, which have indeed contributed to concerning deformations as people pursue self-interest rather than community interest. For instance, governance cryptotokens that represent voting rights in a project were envisaged as a nice vision of democracy, where lots of different people each held a token, sort of a one-man-one-vote equivalent. But what has happened in practice is that those with financial resources simply bought governance tokens from others at an attractive price on the open crypto markets, thereby easily controlling a larger voting share than was envisaged. There are a lot of these examples – where there is money and self-interest on one side and public goods on the other, there will be skirmishes.

What is proposed by the paper is a type of cryptotoken called a 'Soulbound NFT' that holds a collection of personal identifying attributes, like the sort of credentials we have discussed earlier. But there is a critical difference from normal NFTs – they are not transferable and thus can't be sold on markets or even given away (in the next chapter we will dive deeper into NFTs and what they are). They are bound to your... soul. (It turns out that the etymology of the name Soulbound is from a videogame. Give Vitalek some leash here, that was his stomping ground before blockchains.)

Look at the final words of the opening sentence of the Soulbound paper again – 'encoding social relationships of trust'. The token defines who the owner is by dint of what verifiable credentials and attributes are in their wallet. It is a social tapestry that expresses perhaps not all of you, but those pieces that you decide would support and enable relationships of trust. And it can't be transferred to anyone else.

This is not too different from Sovrin in intent, but there are some key differences in implementation.

The first one is that Sovrin and its community started with a top-down approach. What is this thing called personal identity? What is its genesis, history, sociology, philosophy? How does it manifest in individuals and communities? How do we construct a system that captures it in all its anthropological, societal and psychological nuance and complexity?

The Soulbound token paper reverses this approach. It says – here is this neat idea called a Soulbound NFT that can store crypto-verified credentials. This is how we think it should work. We suspect that it is important. This is some of the cool stuff that might happen if it was available. Anyone interested in building something with this?

You might remember – this is exactly how Vitalek launched Ethereum. Here is a neat programming language on top of a blockchain. Here is some cool stuff which I think might be valuable if it was programmed. Anyone interested in building something with it?

The next and most obvious difference is this. Vitalek's name carries more weight in crypto than just about anyone but Satoshi Nakamoto. It is more than his name, though. A suggestion by Vitalek sometimes ends up as a proposal for a new standard on the Ethereum blockchain which, if approved, will become embedded in the fabric of the blockchain, which essentially guarantees a large developer community and hundreds of projects springing up around the new standard. Vitalek's support means traction.

The third difference is that a somewhat bolder and utopian vision of a 'better world' is more poetically articulated by the paper. That of a series of communities and economies that are built on both the trusted identity attributes and transitory identity interactions immutably lodged in an individual's Soulbound wallet, and which can be shared at will. Sure, you can prove that you have a degree to a prospective employer, but you can also find similarly credentialed people around you and build overlapping and perhaps interacting social communities.

The *Bankless* newsletter (a publication of the excellent *Bankless* podcast, previously mentioned) describes it like this:

> When two people have a handshake on their first meeting, that relationship exists only in their fleeting memories. SBTs are an attempt to formalize that handshake on a public blockchain that the rest of the world can witness and verify. In doing so, it allows us to color a person's identity with social context, opening up a world of coordination possibilities that until now wasn't possible without a middleman.
>
> In essence, SBTs are a codification of social capital (i.e., reputation) into formal property ownership. By 'baring our souls', individuals can stake their reputation openly and prove the authenticity of who they say they are.

A perfect example illustrates this point. Given that university degrees are expensive, many people choose less formal avenues for education, like online courses. A collection of these in their SBTs would help give employers a wider set of criteria from which to make hiring decisions.

Vitalek et al. call these decentralized societies, now known as Desocs. There are echoes of old Facebook PR here, where you can build a group of friends based on shared interests. But FB is a sclerotic old beast now. It is not decentralized and, more importantly, anyone can lie about anything on Facebook (or Twitter or others). There is little social trust in these networks because the veracity of its content is not enforced by cryptography or anything else.

There are a slew of other sparkles in this paper. Non-collateralized loans, for instance. One cannot borrow money now on any blockchain by simply promising to pay it back, because everyone is anonymous, by design. The lender has no way of knowing whether the party on the borrowing side is creditworthy or reliable, and so the borrower must lodge collateral. But with Soulbound tokens one could easily check whether a Soulbound wallet has taken previous loans and paid on time, and lenders can lodge credentials testifying to this in the Soulbound wallet of the honest repayers. Opening a way to trust the owner of the wallet and make loans (this would be a massive new market opportunity).

Sovrin belongs to a genre of identity projects called 'verifiable identity' projects (other are Civic, Ontology and Disco), whereas SBTs seek to capture more than your credentials. Your essence perhaps, as the name suggests. There is danger here though – an external party peeping into your wallet could see that you once attended a Trump rally or a Black Lives Matter rally. Conclusions could be drawn and warped, even if you were simply attending out of non-ideological interest.

The authors understand this potential for abuse; there are multiple solutions suggested, drawn from the well of new cryptographic innovations.

Both Sovrin and Soulbound tokens and the many other digital identity initiatives trying to find a home in the world have one thing in common. They are a necessary set of embryonic reactions to the ever increasing immersion of our physical lives into the virtual world, and how this necessarily requires us to carve out multiple versions of ourselves to satisfy new relationships that have formed in the tsunami of new technologies that have washed over us since the arrival of the personal computer in the 1970s.

We were once confined to interactions with family and friends and some strangers and a modest number of institutions. Our interactions have grown massively and chaotically, with new relationships formed by the near infinite swath of digital interactions with apps, avatars, AIs, software agents, augmented realities and real corporeal people we will never actually meet in the flesh. New paradigms become necessary; our old-world physical selves need tools to collate and present just the piece of ourselves that are fit for the many functions to which we are now party.

* * *

Tracey Follows is a well-known and widely-garlanded UK-based futurist, who wrote a terrific book in 2021 called *The Future of You: Can Your Identity Survive 21st-Century Technology?*[22] The book casts a wide net over the subject of personal identity: it is mostly concerned with the dispersion, attenuation, metamorphosis and enhancement of pieces of ourselves into current and future digital and virtual worlds, and who is doing what with those pieces and what control we do or do not have.

Follows builds up her narrative in sharply defined sections – 'Distributing You', 'Knowing You', 'Watching You', 'Creating You', 'Connecting You', 'Replacing You', 'Enhancing You', 'Destroying You'. A tour-de-force of what we are, and what we will be and what different rights and obligations will cleave to all our many identities.

The book starts with the simple but catchy sentence – 'I am not who I say I am.' This is followed by a tale of stolen identity on Facebook – her own. It is the fuel that powers the book. Our identities are fragile, not set, not always controllable, subject to debasement and theft on one side, and change, growth and enhancement on the other. The crypto projects we described here are just the first few small pieces of a bigger identity toolset yet to be manufactured.

Before we jump back into the blockchain, I leave you with her concluding remarks:

In the future, you will still have pseudonymous identities that still express 'you'; you will have avatars which in part create 'you'; you will have a range of credentials that authenticate 'you'; you will have intelligent assistants that expand 'you'; and you will have a digital legacy to preserve 'you'. All of this will still be you, all of this will be congruent with the physical person that is also you...

Chapter 9

NFTs AND THE EMERGENCE OF CRYPTO TITLE REGIMES (AND SNOOP DOGG)

One might expect that our first deep dive into this world would be cryptocurrencies, because those were first out of the gate, the wellspring from which everything else spouted after Satoshi's white paper in 2008. But I am going to start with NFTs because it represents a simpler story, a purer and broader cryptographic expression of ownership, tied to it in surprising ways. And NFTs will serve as fuel for many of the blockchain-supported ecosystems that we will be talking about later in the book.

Most people associate owning an NFT with owning a piece of expensive and sometimes questionable piece of digital art, because that is what was painted in glaring colours across all major global media outlets during 2020 and 2021. I have empathy here, my eyebrows were also raised to my hairline more than a few times during that period, questioning how in the world anyone could be paying that amount for what sometimes amounted to a few blocky kids' characters.

But this is not only incorrect, or at least partially misunderstood, because it is also a tip of a very large iceberg. The NFT story and its relationship to ownership is much deeper and more profound than that.

But first, what is it?

Matt Levine is one of my favourite financial columnists. He writes for Bloomberg, and authors a column called 'Money Stuff', dipping in and out of interesting and current financial matters with irony, humour and refreshing simplicity that never fails to mask his command of important issues. Including, quite often, crypto.

On the matter of NFTs he said something like this (I paraphrase): 'Oh, I get it, it's a receipt' – thus clearing up one of the most deeply held misconceptions about NFTs, which is still widely held.

But before we go there, some light history. Most people with glancing interest in this subject know that NFTs mean 'Non-Fungible Tokens'. Fungibility is an unusual word, which is rarely used in common parlance. If we ignore technical definitions, we can pin it here – fungible items are not unique, they are, for all intents and purposes, interchangeable. Like a dollar bill (sticklers will complain that all dollar bills have a unique serial number, but that is irrelevant in daily usage; they are all considered identical). Non-fungible items live on the other side of this definition – they are unique, one item is definitely distinguishable from another. Like tickets to the opera. They are all tickets, but they have their own individual seat numbers. Or passports – definitely not fungible.

The first attempts at registering 'ownership' on blockchains were experimental and transitory. Soon after the Bitcoin network started operating, an Israeli academic by the name of Meni Rosenfeld wrote a paper that proposed a new use for the Bitcoin blockchain. He raised the concept of a 'Coloured Coin', a token on the Bitcoin blockchain whose function was not to be a currency, but to be representative of something else.

I quote from the paper: '…by carefully tracking the origin of a given Bitcoin, it is possible to color a set of coins to distinguish it from the rest.'

In other words, these Coloured Coins would be non-fungible; they could not be interchanged with coins of another colour. He went on to list some use cases – smart property, deterministic contracts, company stock and other items, foreshadowing just about the entire cryptoverse today. But Rosenfeld did not hold the overarching lens of 'ownership' above his suggestions, even though it hovers there, just out of sight. He preferred to talk about control and transfer – which of course is ownership by any other name.

So what happened to Coloured Coins? Alas, the Bitcoin blockchain was optimized for the Bitcoin cryptocurrency, so its implementation was a little clunky. Extension and enhancement and programmability were not deeply baked in; that had to wait until Ethereum.

But there were a few other precursors to the NFT, the most famous of these being 'Quantum' in 2014. It was an animated video – a series of concentric glowing, shimmering, wavering octagonal shapes, which looked like something from a late 1960s light show. It was created by artist Jennifer McCoy. Her husband Kevin and Anil Dash wrangled tech to 'register' ownership of a domain where the video was available and lodged it on a blockchain called Namecoin.

Why 'registered'? Namecoin was an early blockchain, essentially copied from Bitcoin. It was set up to securely register domain names. You know, like stevenboykeysidley.com. That's what you do with domain names. You register with

The Internet Corporation for Assigned Names and Numbers (ICANN), the non-profit organization that oversees the assignment of both IP addresses and domain names, where they become part of the uber Internet address book in the cloud. Namecoin was an early blockchain platform providing that service, somewhat old and dormant now, overtaken by nimbler players, but still enjoying a quiet immortality out there somewhere. And 'Quantum' is for sale at $7 million.

In any event – a unique piece of art called 'Quantum' and an address on a blockchain that referenced where the art could be found.

An NFT then.

A final historical oddity before we dive deeper. In October 2015 at the first Ethereum developers conference, DEVCON 1, a project called Etheria was launched. The developers minted 437 flat coloured tiles (blue and green). They listed them for sale at $0.43 each. No one was interested. In 2021, when NFTs became a really big deal, interest picked up again, and they were relisted. They sold for $1.4m.

The modern era of NFTs arrived in 2018. A new standard was proposed by William Entriken, Dieter Shirley, Jacob Evans and Nastassia Sachs. It was called by its formal name ERP-721 and it was the first carefully structured definition of what we now more commonly call NFTs. Activity picked up slowly. The first popular NFTs were called Cryptokitties, which started as an experiment where participants could breed, raise, and trade virtual cats with unique genomes. It caught fire, and came close to shutting down the entire Ethereum network when volume spiked by five times as people furiously traded and bred their pets. The cost of certain Cryptokitties soared to over $300,000. They now trade for a fraction of that, some of them below $200. This of course is a well-worn story – hair-raising prices, and then a big crater, and then a semblance of normalcy.

In 2020/2021 the top blew off the industry. It had gone from curiosity to lurid headlines in a few years. But the NFT story was always going to be about more than that. Nestling at its core was a new idea, which is only now starting to spread into the rest of the cryptoverse.

* * *

Let's return to the comment – 'Oh I get it, it's a receipt' – for a moment, and explain the semantic confusion around NFTs. An NFT is indeed a very secure receipt, not counterfeitable or changeable, secured by fancy cryptography, controllable and transferable only by using a private key. Or, if one wants to get all hifalutin, one could say it's a tad more than a receipt, it's a digital title deed.

The misconception is that most buyers of NFTs think that they bought the thing, the underlying art or asset whatever. No they didn't. Whether they actually 'own' the underlying thing is another matter, it is perhaps programmed in the NFT code, or some other fine print of sale. Like outright ownership of IP, or copyright, or partial ownership, or temporary ownership, or just viewing rights or some other hybrid. But they bought the receipt. It turns out that ownership of the NFT usually does not give copyright, but then this is true of the physical world too. Making this real *caveat emptor* territory and a fertile revenue stream for lawyers (as we discussed in an earlier chapter) as they battle the fine nuances of buying-the-thing vs buying-the-thing-that-says-you-own-the-thing, and the mysteries of property law. Amy Whitaker from New York

University wrote an article in which she neatly sidestepped the question, comparing the tension between abundance of digital copies and the single digital NFT receipt and called it 'aura' of ownership. Her quote is lovely:

> A singular feature of NFTs as art is the way that they function as public goods – memes circulating on the internet that are non-excludable and non-rivalrous in consumption, that is, impossible to gatekeep enjoyment and possible to be viewed by many at the same time. But then the NFT or certificate takes this public-good nature (the lack of digital scarcity) and allows it to function as a singular and saleable object. In this way, NFTs replace the aura of the original artwork with the aura of ownership.[23]

There is an obvious question which we should quickly ask and answer. Why, in October 2021 would someone have paid over $3.4 million for an NFT describing the piece of digital art *Bored Ape #8817* – a graphic of a primate with an earring, a propellor cap and streamer between their lips? Or any of the other wild prices paid across the many NFT markets that cropped up in the first few years of this decade? The answer is, I don't know. That's what they paid. I also don't know why someone paid $91 million for a little stainless-steel sculpture of a rabbit by Jeff Koons that I wouldn't have looked at twice had I seen it at a garage sale. And that had nothing to do with crypto. Go figure.

There are jpgs of this and other Bored Apes as well as millions of other NFT-tethered digital content all over the web. What's to stop someone from bringing up a graphic of *Bored Ape #8817* on their screen and saving the image?

Taking possession of a perfect copy, so to speak. Nothing. But that person does not own the NFT bound to it and the bragging and selling rights which come from ownership. Or at least the 'aura' of ownership.

There are, by one recent measurement, over 80 million NFT-tethered works of digital art available on NFT marketplaces, but, as you can imagine, almost all of them lie sadly neglected, and the majority of the few that do trade fetch less than $200. The halcyon days when a thirteen-year-old can sell his scribble for $60K are gone (true story).

The entire value market is now dominated by celebrities, brands and corporations (punctured only occasionally by a brash newcomer or fine artist). Like Adidas, Lamborghini, Coca-Cola, Nike, Louis Vuitton, Samsung, Pepsi, McDonald's, Burger King, Ray-Ban. And Eminem, Snoop Dogg, Grimes, Paris Hilton, Kevin Hart, LeBron James, Justin Timberlake, etc. Every day brings another brand into the fold, all seemingly falling over each other to join the party before it is too late. My news feed includes a number of NFT news sites. It is a firehose: multiple announcements every day, which leads to the nagging question, will there one day be an NFT for... everything? Perhaps, and there are futurists who certainly bat this thought around.

I find this all a little depressing, especially after reading about a toilet paper company called Charmin that has jumped on the bandwagon. Perhaps it is the co-opting of something that was fresh and new by the usual suspects with access to means and influence. But my feelings notwithstanding, something even deeper has emerged in all of this quasi-lemming like behaviour.

* * *

The Bored Ape Yacht Club (or BAYC, as it is commonly known) has become sort of a bellwether for the NFT industry. 10,000 images were minted by Yuga Labs on 23rd April 2021 by four pseudonymous creators, all of whom have now been outed (or have outed themselves). They were sold out within a week. Their price was about $180; they sell for over $100,000 each at the time of writing.

There is not much deep coverage about the strategic plans that Yuga Labs had at the time, but I think that we can be fairly certain that they had no expectation of the depth and energy of the public buying frenzy. I am also pretty sure they never had a business plan and a grand vision beyond selling out their collection and perhaps making some money. But there is something in the name of the project that gives away perhaps a glimmer of what was to come, perhaps what they talked about as they put it all together – the Bored Ape Yacht Club.

Club.

This is where the ownership deepens. Yes, the ape visages are fun, I suppose, for those who can afford it and like to use it as identifying social media pictures mixed in with a little bragging here and there. But what really turbocharged the NFT was that it migrated from owning the graphic to owning membership in an exclusive club (or 'gated token community' – insider jargon for club).

This turns out to be a much bigger deal than simply buying an NFT of an artwork or other media file. If you own a Bored Ape you now have permanent membership in the 'Bored Ape Yacht Club'; (visions of restricted entry elitism float by on gentle harbour waves). So what? I'll tell you what: ostentatiously catered meet-ups in NY, California,

UK, Japan. Discord groups swapping valuable tips about crypto and what to buy and sell. And in June 2022, 'Ape Fest', a festival that included performances from Eminem, Snoop Dogg, LCD Soundsystem and Amy Schumer. Other VIP events. Oh and free 'air drops' of secondary BAYC NFTs like Mutant Apes and membership to the Bored Ape Kennel Club where you can mint pets for your Ape. Early access to ApeCoins, a cryptocurrency carrying the brand name. And probably most importantly, the surge of new on-chain/off-chain partnerships like a limited edition sneaker by Adidas. Oh, and a real three-part movie funded by Coinbase (where you can submit your Ape for casting).

You can easily imagine where this is headed. Your ownership of the NFT includes rights to membership of an exclusive community which includes celebrities, which only increases its value, which brings in more aspirant members paying ever higher prices, which brings in real brand collaborations, and more celebrities, and, and...

An article in the *Harvard Business Review* by Steve Kaczynski and Scott Duke Kominers sums it up:

> Thus owning an NFT effectively makes you an investor, a member of a club, a brand shareholder, and a participant in a loyalty program all at once. At the same time, NFTs' programmability supports new business and profit models – for example, NFTs have enabled a new type of royalty contract, whereby each time a work is resold, a share of the transaction goes back to the original creator.[24]

So we can talk about boring old title regimes all we want, but really, who cares if we can go and hang out with Eminem and

Snoop Dogg in our new exclusive NFT-owners-only Adidas
sneakers at the club.

* * *

There are a few more matters to mention before we move on.

I wanted to start the journey into ownership ecosystems
with NFTs because they represent something broader than
cryptocurrencies. A cryptocurrency gives you ownership
of a fungible token that represents pure value like Bitcoin,
each indistinguishable from the other. There are thousands
of these cryptocurrencies, but I would hazard that less than
ten of them have any real sustainable value (no matter what
their price at any given moment). But there are millions of
different NFTs, and all of them represent something unique
which may have value, may have had value, and may one
day have value or, more interestingly, may have no interest
in attracting any value at all. The NFT is first and foremost
a title deed. Whether there is value in the underlying asset to
which it is tethered is secondary.

This gives it a much larger canvas. Consider the NFT that
represents the data describing my car trips on some future
navigation app. It has value to me, a history of where I have
travelled. It is not monetary value that interests me, but it is
a priceless personal memoir. It may have monetary value to
an advertiser, but selling it to them may be of zero interest,
or even offensive, to me.

How flexible is this new-fangled representation of ownership, the NFT? Earlier we mentioned the establishment of
the first NFT standard on the Ethereum blockchain, called
ERC-721. NFTs and ERC-721 tokens are often used inter-
changeably, which is reckless and inaccurate. ERC-721 tokens

are only one expression of the larger subject of NFTs. There are others out there in the cryptosphere – ERC-721A, ERC-721Enumerable, ERC-1155 and certainly more to come. But it is the principle of a blockchain-secured NFT that is more important than the various instantiations now living on various blockchains. The principle is that of *programmable* ownership, sometimes called elastic ownership. Ownership whose clauses and rules and internal logic can morph and redefine depending on an essentially infinite range of conditions. I own this today, my wife owns the thing tomorrow, my best friend owns it when it rains and, if it's sold, 5% goes automatically to my favourite charity. That sort of thing.

So NFTs are, in principle, infinitely flexible, while the current reigning ERC-721 is less so, having some built-in constraints. But the more generic vision of an NFT is that if the terms of ownership can be imagined, then it can be coded, deployed, secured and executed on the blockchain. For example, in our previous chapter we talked about Vitalek's 'Soulbound NFT'. It was imagined into existence in a long paper, and will surely be formalized and documented and seeped into the fabric of yet unconceived applications. So too for some of the blockchain-borne structures we will talk about later in this book, many of them underpinned by some form of NFT architecture.

I want to end the chapter on NFTs with some new threads that have begun to appear, confounding factors that point to future battlegrounds. There is a project called NFTfi, started by the South African-born Stephen Young. The proposition is simple and enticing – we will lend you cryptocurrency against the value of your NFT. So let's say a BAYC owner needs money for her child's college education. She paid $20,000 for her

Bored Ape, which is now trading at $100,000. She hands over her NFT as collateral to NFTfi, who agrees to lend her some lesser amount (to protect against price crashes), like $66,000 million in some cryptocurrency, say USDC. She then cashes out the USDC, wires the money to her bank, and pays the college fees. If the price goes up, she never has to pay it back, until she reclaims her NFT, which she doesn't have to do. If the price of her Bored Ape crashes, she gets automatically liquidated at $66,000.

The confounding factor is this. If you are a regulator trying to make sense of this, would you see the NFT as a title deed, or a financial asset? It is after all being used just like money-based collateral in a bank. Indeed, towards the end of 2022, the IRS suddenly woke up to this fact and expanded its language of 'virtual currency' to 'digital asset', specifically including NFTs. Or, given that its underlying value is a piece of art, is it some other sort of asset, like a property, which can be mortgaged? And how do you repossess the thing if something bad happens?

Here's another. Let's say someone mints 1,000 NFTs of some underlying digital file, distinguishable from each other by, say, a 'print' number, and that the NFTs became so ubiquitous and popular that they are actually used to buy stuff. Is this collection of title deeds now nothing more than a currency, requiring all manner of regulatory straightjackets?

And another. There is a genre of digital art called generative art. It is art that is constantly changing under the baton of dynamic instructions, like time of day, or simply every time it is viewed. This 'baton' is under programmatic control, either within the NFT itself, or in the digital file that defines the artwork. The resulting artwork is not only constantly changing, but it is also entirely unpredictable. What then does a person own when they own the NFT? Clearly not the artwork at a point in time, which cannot be pinned down. The code then, perhaps. But there are legal problems there too. All of the stuff in crypto is open-source, so anyone can copy the code, perhaps make minimal changes and build their own fountain of generating art. Legal hazard indeed.

The matter of what rights accrue to the NFT owner in the face of all this ambiguity has attracted considerable attention. In September 2022 the venture capital company a16z released a free licence framework called Can't Be Evil (cocking a snook at Google's original and much maligned mantra 'Don't be evil').

It is inspired by the well-known Creative Commons CC0 toolkit (meaning 'no copyright reserved'), which has often been used when creators completely waive copyright, allowing anyone to do anything with their work. The Can't Be Evil[25] toolkit seeks to address buyer misunderstanding – the licence spells out exactly what rights the buyer does and doesn't have. For instance, it has check boxes for each of 'copy/display', 'modify/adapt', 'hate-speech revocation', 'commercial use' and 'sublicense'. This can only indicate a maturing of a confusing space, and a new focus on buyer's rights.

Still, NFTs are a wildly mutating breed. Experiments and projects and launches and use cases multiply like fruit flies. Some dying out, some surviving, some interbreeding with others to make something new.

Only the bravest, or perhaps the most foolish, will try to predict where or when this will all settle, and in what form. What objects and artefacts in our human societies cry out for the protection of secure NFT ownership and the security of mathematical locks and keys? Which of them offers an option of monetization? What cries out to be left alone? What will best use this thing called non-fungible tokens? Who will abuse it? Where are the ethicists and philosophers who will guide NFTs journey from messy experiment to human right?

In the following chapters we will see the future of NFTs in action across a wide spectrum of human activities. It is a creature of many splendours.

Chapter 10

DEFI – OWNING OUR
FINANCIAL JOURNEYS

In 2020 I started writing with co-writer Simon Dingle the book I mentioned in the Introduction. It was called *Beyond Bitcoin: Decentralised Finance and The End of Banks*. At the time Defi had just burst onto the crypto scene, an inevitable consequence of Ethereum, the smart contract and a lumbering and well-protected industry of financial institutions, some of whose decades-old services and overweight architectures were ripe for disruption.

This included banks and exchanges and insurance companies, among others. Some disruption had already started about ten years earlier when the fastest-moving of these institutions started their 'digital transformation' journeys, which was mainly a fancy way of saying that customer services were moved onto mobile devices with veneers of self-service. But the internal guts of the institutions did not move much. There was some migration of ancient data centres into the cloud, some new clever marketing campaigns that used social media, some cost-savings arising from newer software architectures.

But as a customer of these institutions you saw much the same set of stolid services – a limited set of products offering deposits, loans, transfers, credit cards, insurance packages and ability to trade regulated assets on exchanges. The most cynical of us would have viewed these industries as near-cartels, finding little to distinguish one bank from another, one insurance company from another. Competitive differentiators were few and far between, and new services blared their wares much more loudly than was warranted.

Towards the middle of the second decade of the millennium a new group of brash upstarts appeared, all lumped under the rubric of 'Fintechs'. But again, these were mainly smart customer-acquisition hooks, better customer services, self-service upgrades, simpler interfaces. There were some new services, like remittance and mobile payments, but nothing much changed at the back-ends other than newer core banking software ecosystems; an upgrade rather than anything truly revolutionary.

During our research into the drivers for Defi we kept bumping our heads into the same wall, which was the asymmetry of power between these institutions and their customers. It was almost feudal, with the landowners living warm and protected in the manor house, and us in the outside chill, with few options to object or disrupt on offer. Most of us never stopped to think about it. Why were we paying exactly these premiums and how were they calculated? Were the interest on loans too high, or the loans on deposits too low? How did we know? How were the credit card fees or exchange brokerage fees set and why? Why were the bank execs paid so much? Were shareholder dividends unfair to their customers? These were not questions for us; we accepted them meekly and found that the financial institution around the corner was offering much the same thing.

The litany of uneasiness did not stop there. Rich customers were treated better than poor ones; they were ranked in terms of the profit that they brought to the bank. Our money disappeared for days at a time, with no interest paid, while a thing called 'settlement' occurred. The dictates of compliance made signing up with these institutions, or moving from one to another a dispiriting process. And people without proper credit or enough cash were not included in the banking system at all.

Most importantly it did not feel like we had control. The financial journeys we were offered were owned by them, these megaliths. We were herded like sheep through well-trodden product routes, our money handed over to be scraped and scalped on its way to executing its function. In short, we did not own the journey and once we were en route it was hard to escape.

None of this was malicious or malevolent. It was efficient for the financial institutions, who more than anything needed our trust. Without that, we wouldn't hand over our money. And so they constructed manageable walled gardens with a constrained set of offerings running on opaque internals. The very constraints that were dictated to their customers made it easy for them to ensure their trustworthiness. Too much flexibility may have brought them loss of control and unacceptable risk.

None of this was new or remarkable in 2015. That was the world of financial institutions we have lived under since the Medici banking empires built in Italy in the 1300s.

* * *

Enter blockchain.

When Ethereum and its smart contract programming capability was unleashed, a number of techno entrepreneurs looked around for projects to explore that could offer something better, perhaps even new and unprecedented. There was surely material motivation; these founders likely had as much desire as anyone to make money, but many of the early builders were indeed interested in 'public goods', zealous in their ideology to level playing fields and topple embedded power structures. In retrospect, perhaps I should be more jaded, with the news awash with ill-advised projects falling over in 2022, dodgy founders, and some great disappointments in the discipline of basic risk management.

But the very early first-born Defi projects were built from more innocent motives. By 2017 the crypto universe had started to attract significant capital and enough liquidity to rebuild many financial-institutional-type services within the walls of crypto. It was almost a sandbox for financial experimentation, using cryptocurrencies (of which there were many by 2017) as raw fodder, outside of the regulation and legacy of the outside world.

Rune Christenson started MakerDAO in 2017, the first successful lend/borrow Defi product, allowing deposits and loans in different cryptocurrencies (and inventing the first stablecoin DAI along the way). Hayden Adams built the first non-regulated decentralized peer-to-peer crypto exchange called Uniswap, which made it dramatically less expensive to execute trades than on any equivalent real-world exchange. Andre Cronje built the 'world's smartest savings account' called Yearn, which hopped in real-time from crypto project to crypto project looking for the best yields, like a crypto money market on steroids. Hugh Karp built a blockchain-based insurance company called Nexus Mutual to mitigate risk within crypto projects. Michael Egorov started Curve, which basically invented algorithmic liquidity using a technique now called an Algorithmic Market Maker (AMM). Derivatives markets were developed, offering synthetic pricing of real-world assets, at lower cost and with fewer restrictions than real-world equivalents. Unique new financial products popped up, with no precedent in the legacy industry.

This went on and on, project after project, all reimagining part of the traditional financial system and rebuilding on the blockchain, pretty much ignoring the institutional memory of hundreds of years of tradfi and certainly ignoring the just awakening beast of regulation.

And then, inevitably, two worlds collided.

Many of these projects required liquidity, that great grease of finance, to operate effectively. So all manner of incentives (sometimes called 'token emissions', sometimes more ironically called 'bribes') were offered by the projects to entice investors to hand over their crypto capital into project liquidity or trading pools. Sometimes 'bribes' were paid for simply using the service. For instance, a project would say: give us your money. In return we will give you a publicly tradable special token which allows you to vote on the future direction of the project, sort of like a mini-board of directors seat. These incentive tokens, trading on their own immature public markets, sometimes rocketed up in value, attracting ever increasing money from investors and traders, and yielding impossible double and triple and quadruple percentage annual returns.

The collision of the two worlds was here. People in the non-crypto outside world, grimly looking at their sub-1% returns in the early 2020s tradfi banks, saw an opportunity to make 10, 20, 50, 100% returns within the walls of crypto. So they opened accounts at crypto exchanges and the great sound of traditional money whooshing from tradfi into Defi projects could be heard. Of course the returns were not sustainable, simple maths would show that 100% return a year would suck the wealth out of the planet quite quickly – it was not feasible in anything but the very short term. The entire enterprise was riding on the back of the inflation of secondary Defi markets and funded by investors who hoped that their choice of Defi project would quickly make them rich with the incentive tokens that they had bought, or in some cases, been given.

Our book dug into a number of these projects, how they were started, who started them, what their incentive structures were, how they worked beneath the hood. The northern hemisphere summer of 2020 became known as 'Defi Summer', as multiple projects exploded onto the scene, each one barking their wares into faces of a somewhat bewildered but enthusiastic audience, many eager to believe promises built on jargon and sand.

By 2021 Defi was in full swing, but regulators had started circling, sober voices had started whispering about risk, and solid projects like MakerDAO, Compound, Aave, Yearn, Uniswap, Synthetix, dYdX, Nexus Mutual, Curve and others tried their best to avoid the contagion of rushed or poorly architected competitors. Towards the middle of 2022 things collapsed spectacularly. A project called Terra Luna crumbled under a poorly conceived 'tokenomic' (or underlying economic) set of assumptions, losing over $40 billion in a few weeks, and bringing down a host of entangled projects who had borrowed from the entreprise. It was carnage. Many innocent investors got hurt (or ruined), regulators fumed, promising fire and brimstone, most major media gloated and many 'I-told-you-sos' were heard around the world.

And yet.

Defi has survived, largely intact. Its centre has held firm. The big reputable projects we previously mentioned barely blinked under the sudden terrified outflow of scared investors' capital. The smart contracts did not panic; they are code after all, they continued to operate smoothly. Projects offering eye-watering annual returns retreated or disappeared. What had happened was no less than a cleaning-up of the gene pool, a rejection of deformed experiments, whether well- or ill-intended in the first place. And as we slid towards the end of 2022 a new burnish arrived. It was called 'Real Yield', a replacement for the wild speculation of incentive tokens and secondary markets. There are a number of players (like Umami and GMX) who understand the damage that unsustainable returns have done, and who have built new Defi ecosystems that share 'protocol fees', using that as ballast for attractive yields. What are 'protocol yields'? Well, it means taking the capital and washing it through vibrant projects, like derivative markets and other exotic instruments. Hmm. We shall see. But I am buoyed by what Alex O'Donnell, CEO of Umami said in an interview.[26]

The DeFi ecosystem is still in a place where it is trying to win trust from users and there's many good reasons why users don't have complete trust... in that context, showing users through your actions that you are going to make good on the promise that if they hold your token, they will capture a share of the value that you're creating, is really critical.

Let's pause here and relook at the ownership component of Defi. On the one side, we have a millennia-old financial system. They take possession of our funds and offer services in return, putting our capital to work in various ways, for which we get a return or a convenience. They are trustworthy, they don't lose our funds, and they generally perform the functions which they advertise. They also extract rent to perform their function, not a problem in and of itself (most are, after all, profit-making entities), unless that rent is too high. Which many of the innovators in Defi claim.

Moreover, they take ownership of their customers in toto. Their customers' personal details, their passwords and the nature of the relationship, over which they have almost complete control. And of course their customer's money, which in principle is only under their custody (and regulated as such), but in practice can be misappropriated within a labyrinthian system that we do not understand, and which is sometimes manipulated by bad actors within their systems. We play by their rules, they do not play by ours – that is the game. And if something goes wrong, lost transactions or misplaced funds or shoddy service, recourse is difficult and onerous, and entirely the burden of the customer, who must report it and hope for mitigation. And the financial paths which are offered to us are entirely theirs – terms and conditions, interfaces, products, support ecosystems.

The relationship is starkly asymmetrical.

On the other side there is Defi. At least in its most ideological version it sought to turn this relationship on its head, or at least give it some balance. Capital providers and traders and investors could enter one of many Defi service providers without friction, and transact, deposit and withdraw in seconds, with absolute certainty about the transparency of the underlying product, given the open-source nature of their underlying smart contracts. No bad human actors could roam the system secretly misappropriating your funds, and you were free to shut down your relationship with a project and move to a new one with little inconvenience or effort, often within minutes. There were no shareholders to pay dividends, no large data centres to be amortised, no expensive security processes, no fancy buildings, no opaque transfer of risk, no executive salaries and armies of employees to be paid.

The customer, you and I, were given a level of control over these journeys that were utterly absent in the legacy financial world.

It worked this way for a while. But like all things that seek to entice greed to give up its hunger and give fairness a bite, things did not always go as planned. Hackers, grifters and hucksters found their way in and exploited bugs and lax controls. Your crypto, as much as it was yours, was often pledged into the liquidity and staking pools which were attacked, drained and evaporated under the misfortune of bugs and criminals. Specialized incentive cryptotokens could not sustain their initial meteoric rises and slumped. Although we need to point out that these problems did not occur in the underlying blockchain, mainly Ethereum: it was other points in the ecosystem – the smart contracts, the underlying economic controls and the interfaces and portals to the real world.

Not all contracts and interfaces, of course, but enough to bruise the trust that has been such a core part of the block-chain value proposition.

One needs to consider that in order to use these services, one needs to transfer crypto from our own wallets into a smart Defi contract somewhere, so that it can be deployed into service on our behalf. For example, promising attractive annual rates of return while it remains under control of the smart contract. At the very point at which we do this (transferring our money), we have given up secure ownership of our tokens, and trustingly handed them over to a piece of software, a smart contract, lodged on a blockchain. The blockchain may be bulletproof, but not the smart contract. To put it more simply, we have ceded temporary ownership of wealth on the promise of some future benefit to us.

So while we may have gained some of the control of the journey we wish to take, at least in comparison to traditional finance, part of that journey requires temporarily relinquishing control of our money, just as it does in tradfi. And so trust again raises its virtuous and expressionless head. It is a much simpler matter to relinquish control of tokens to a wallet or address that is lodged on a blockchain whose fairly concise mathematical security has been tested and scrutinized for over a decade, like Bitcoin. It is an entirely different matter to hand your tokens over to a more complex software program. Even the best of those programs, which are often audited and tested by third-party security companies, are sometimes subject to bugs and vulnerabilities – it is the nature of software programs. They need the maturing of time to prove their mettle. Like wine, they get better with age, or at least more trustworthy.

* * *

Where does this leave the ownership narrative? On closer inspection we find this:

Ownership is ceded constantly and widely in all areas of human endeavour, if only temporarily and always with conditions, explicit or implicit. I lend you the keys to my car – the conditions (usually unspoken) are that you bring my car back undamaged. If you breach those conditions because ownership was temporarily out of my control, then I need to find recourse – my insurance company, you, or sometimes none at all. This happens in all sorts of relationships of convenience, commercial or personal. We require a voluntary and temporary loosening of ownership security in order to interact in society. It works beautifully where we can trust on the return of the owned item, undebased. But we never can do that fully, not even in the best of circumstances, like the loan of a book to a dear friend, the most fraught of my less substantial trust risks.

And here we must give credence to the traditional financial system which Defi is seeking to challenge. We trust big-brand banks, exchanges and insurance companies because of their track record and regulation compliance. We may baulk at the rent extracted, we may chafe at the fraught reversals of mistakes, or the sudden changes in fees, or the long customer support hold times, but we generally do not have ownership of our goods wrenched from our grasp. There are few Defi initiatives that approach this level of trustworthiness. At least not yet. They will either need to stand the test of time or have the backstop of insurance or other protections before they can fully compete with legacy systems.

There are a number of caveats here. There are also celebrated institutional failures in our recent history – track record is not everything: we remember Lehman Bros and AIG. Banks in less regulated geographies have often fared less well, bad internal actors have stolen funds, governments have closed commercial banks accounts, as in Cyprus in 2013. And we have not yet discussed the elephant in the room, the bank of banks, which are the national central banks. We will save this subject for another chapter.

* * *

Secure ownership and associated property rights sit close to the core of civil life, but the ability to interact in a community requires ecosystems of temporary ownership and reciprocal trust. Here is where the promise of the trapdoor function and its eventual expression on the blockchain finds both challenge and opportunity.

How do we use crypto to tie down ecosystems of 'temporary' ownership which are transferred between peoples and parties in order to facilitate relationships of mutual interest? Lend/borrow is the most obvious of these; it has been at the centre of finance for hundreds of years. And it is a fairly simple matter in a bank. They commit to settling the lend and borrow ledger on your behalf, and do the critically important work of credit-checking the borrower. It does not always work, of course – people and entities default for all sorts of reasons – but the bank stands by its commitment to make good.

This leads us down a sidetrack. Loans require that the borrower is able to repay. This is the guts of 'credit' calculation. Does the borrower have the ability to pay in the future, to service the loan? Is there a reasonable probability of future earnings or income? Has there ever been a default? Is there collateral lodged in the case of default? Is the collateral easily liquidated? Many data points are assembled and thrown into a pot, and the loan is approved or not. Collateral and future estimates of income or cash flow sit at the centre of these calculations.

Banks know how to do this. Defi is still learning. The first Defi lend/borrow algorithms required over-collateralization (meaning you put up more than you borrow), in some cases as much as 50%, to protect against plummeting crypto-asset prices. New projects have started which look to other ways of scoring credit without collateral, but they are still immature and finding their feet. One of these is Rocifi, which has tossed in a new and intriguing idea. They say, we don't know for sure if the borrower is creditworthy, but the blockchain is entirely open for inspection. So the lender can, at his or her option, make a decision to lend cryptotokens based on the previous history of transactions of the prospective lender on the blockchain. The credit decision (and risk) is now entirely in the wheelhouse of the lender, not the smart contract facilitating the movement of tokens between them. It is called blockchain-based peer-to-peer lending – it is potentially a gigantic market, especially for the financially excluded who have no access to loan capital, depending on the accuracy of credit-scoring assistance provided by the smart contract.

End of sidebar – back to ownership and blockchain and Defi.

Eagle-eyed readers will notice that this chapter was headed – 'Defi – Owning Our Financial Journeys.' Yes, well, that was a bit disingenuous. Defi has allowed us to regain some control over the journeys our money takes, mainly by offering us a smorgasbord of blockchain services far more sumptuous and exotic and often faster and cheaper than those on offer by the traditional financial services industry. Yes, the services are underpinned by crypto, we hold secure ownership of our assets until we transfer them out to go to work for us, but there is no fundamental blockchain cryptography that protects the single end-to-end meandering of your money as it moves through temporary custodianship of smart contracts and the entangled relationships of convenience that must exist for Defi to do its work.

For that we need utterly impenetrable smart contracts. And as we know from the ongoing flow of security patches we need to install on our laptop and mobile operating systems, it takes a very long time to be 'impenetrable'. One could make that claim for the safety of a token sitting at an address on a blockchain like Bitcoin or Ethereum, but it is less certain with smart contracts, which are just computer programs. The longer and more complex the smart contract, the more uncertain its armour. What is the Defi industry to do with the albatross of its immaturity?

There are really only a few options. The most interesting of all is crypto-insurance, as exemplified by Nexus Mutual and others, where smart contract users can pay a small premium to the crypto insurance company to ensure that they are compensated in the case of a problem. The second is government insurance – there are many regulatory battles to be had before this happens, and as we know, even government insurance has borders and limitations. And there are miles to walk before governments understand how to regulate in this space.

And then, of course, there is time. The financial industry has the advantage here, hundreds of years; but there is no metric that I know of that says 'this smart contract is safe enough'. When that happens we will have a coherent single set of security rails for the entire journey of your crypto through the Defi system.

When that happens, traditional finance will suddenly make friends with Defi.

Chapter 11

CRYPTOCURRENCIES –
THE ORIGINAL GANGSTER

I was living in Los Angeles in the early 1990s, just prior to the emergence of the public Internet, but which was already bristling with early energy. I was on the computer animation side of technology, taken with the intersection of art and science that it represented and enthused by what it may become. I worked with a lot of young developer-artists at the time, and they were poking at the Internet with great excitement. Even further on the horizon was a more exotic species who had started a movement that flitted by me in conversations among the developers in the animation studio. I pretty much ignored it, but I was amused by their really cool name.

Cypherpunks.

Who were they? It was a group of about 700 crypto enthusiasts who communicated with each other in the early to mid-90s using early versions of electronic mail. Much has been written about this group, but essentially everyone that had anything to do with the development of Bitcoin has brushed against them, either as enthusiastic contributors or occasional chirpers or lurkers. The nature of the exchanges ranged from technical to political to philosophical, from civil discourse to insults and putdowns. Some used pseudonyms, others used their real names. But if there was a common thread, it was the desire to protect personal privacy, particularly from governments and other unwelcome institutional eyes.

There is actually a document called *The Cypherpunks Manifesto*,[27] written in 1993 by one of the core members of this group, Eric Hughes. In it he wrote:

> Privacy is necessary for an open society in the electronic age... We cannot expect governments, corporations, or other large, faceless organisations to grant us privacy... We must defend our own privacy if we expect to have any... Cypherpunks write code. We know that someone has to write software to defend privacy, and... we're going to write it.

There are many books and scholarly articles about this period. It is fertile territory for studying the groundwork that was laid for the first cryptocurrency, Bitcoin. But the line from their urgent and very vocal defence of privacy to our 'secure ownership' proposition is direct and simple. We want to ensure our privacy, they agreed. Which leads to this proposition – the best way to do that is to ensure secure ownership of our possessions and ourselves, without which privacy walls are thin, even porous.

It is ironic that an industry this young already has lore, legends, pioneers and elders, many of them veterans of the Cypherpunk movement. Some of these OGs spun off into other areas of privacy and cryptography, but others found themselves pulled into cryptocurrency, the first blockchain use case. Names like David Chaum, Adam Back, Wei Dai, Nick Szabo, Hal Finney. And cryptocurrencies still dominate the public imagination, including regulators and media. If you had to compare column inches between cryptocurrencies and, say, DAOs or Web3, well...

Of course, there are good reasons for why cryptocurrencies have taken pole position as an application. Money is the most immediate and urgent of our concerns, up there with family, health, career and community. But the public Internet had been around for fifteen years by the time Satoshi wrote his white paper. Why was money so late to the Internet game?

There is a long historical road on which dreams of alternative money have travelled, sometimes called 'private money'. In the middle of the nineteenth century there were 8,000 such currencies in the US alone, issued by what were called 'wildcat' banks. It did not last long – the federal government put a stop to it in 1863 via the National Bank Act. Other countries have had similar spasms of private cash. They didn't last.

With the advent of mainframe computing in the 1950s and its wizards in the ivory halls of academic research, many theoretical discussions were had as to the efficacy and mechanics of using bits to fulfil the function of cash, payment, money, value. None of them came to much until the invention of private key cryptography, which we have celebrated, and the work our friend David Chaum and colleagues discussed in earlier chapters. He went directly to the heart of the digital currency opportunity both academically and commercially.

In 1983 he was the lead author on a paper called 'Blind Signatures for Untraceable Payments', its title revealing an early interest in the application of cryptography to money. A side note – co-author on the paper was Ron Rivest, one of the original scientists behind RSA, source of the little yellow lock next to your URL on your browser.

The paper was one of the early bricks that was used to build the blockchain industry, because it described a way to use digital signatures and other crypto techniques to shield payments from third-party scrutiny and so to preserve the privacy of payers and payees, both principles that were embraced by the blockchain.

He also solved one of the great Achilles heels of digital money, which was the ability to detect and reject 'double spend'. Previous attempts at replicating cash and payment ecosystems in software had run into this wall. Bits are easy to copy. If money is to be made of bits, what is to stop a payer from making multiple copies of his money and spending it many times? It was a major breakthrough that greased the wheels for Satoshi's paper (or indeed Chaum's white paper, if he is one and the same person).

A final note about Chaum. He put all of his original thinking into a first-of-kind cryptocurrency he called ecash, and formed a commercial company called Digicash in 1995 to bring it to market. The company did not survive and Chaum left in 1999; it was premature, all the pieces that ended up in Satoshi's paper had not yet smoothly engaged with each other into an end-to-end working system.

The preceding paragraphs lightly touch on some of the technical problems that had to be solved to generate a digital machine that could, at minimum, replicate how money worked in the real world.

But there were other matters that both impeded and accelerated the arrival of self-owned digital money.

The first of these was the Internet itself, the only logical choice for a communication network that could carry global transactions. The first glimmerings of technology to support communications between networked computers started in the 1960s, and led to an early network that connected a few US Universities called ARPANET in the 1970s. ARPANET was funded by the US Defense Agency Research Program (DARPA), whose interest in this new area of technology was, unsurprisingly, to secure government and military computers from attack, even in the case of nuclear war. They wanted a way for computers to keep running no matter what. The Internet provided that architecture. A dead computer could simply result in network traffic being rerouted through other nodes.

Why was this important to the emergence of cryptocurrencies? Or at least the timing thereof? Because the Internet was originally funded by government money, and they were strict about not allowing profit-driven entities to exploit their generosity. No commerce was allowed on their network; it was strictly research funding. So no one really had a reason to spend a whole lot of time thinking about Internet money in the 70s and 80s, at least beyond a group of core researchers. Many other standards and protocols were given loving attention – file transfer (FTP), hyperlinks (HTTP), graphic formats like PNG and JPG, video formats, audio formats, browsers, email standards.

And then suddenly the Internet was open to the public and to the profit motive. Because there was no standard for Internet money or digital cash, the only source of funding for aspirant Internet entrepreneurs and website purveyors was advertisers, who paid using traditional systems, not directly on the Internet. Soon after, when security and powerful encryption technologies became robust and standardized, credit cards and then bank transfers started using the Internet as a carrier. But not new – mere simulacra from a legacy age.

By 2008 there was still no 'native' Internet money, while video, audio, VOIP and other standards were now part of the internal language of Internet applications. Internet money was conspicuously absent, a late-starter.

There is another more squishy reason why cryptocurrency may have arrived so much later than the other natives. Just a theory. The Internet had opened up a world of information to anyone who sought it. The world had become a louder place, many opinions raising their voices to be heard. Many news stories competing for eyes and a chaos of information suddenly swimming by, leaving people a little bewildered, possibly, by the widening landscape. Throw into to this mix some of the calamitous stories of our time – wobbly economic systems, 9/11, climate change, the Iraq War, and we might posit that it had a deleterious effect on the average user's confidence in the future, the beginning of an accelerating loss of trust in institutions, which continues today. Institutions like central banks.

Throw into this mix a couple of smart developers and cryptographers and the arrival of a monetary system whose future was secured by maths, whose value could not be debased by bad human decisions (like the age-old money printers of bad governments), whose zeitgeist was privacy and security, and you perhaps have a perfect storm, something whose time has arrived at the exact point where there were enough people to accept it as a defence against power. 2009 and the years succeeding this seemed to converge in time and purpose.

Reading some of the original contributors to the crypto experiments like the Bitcoin blockchain, one finds this worldview sometimes hovering in sight. We do not trust our banks and governments, you can hear them whisper and sometimes roar, surely we can do better than that? Surely we can create a tool that allows us to *own* and exchange our own money, free from constraint?

The first sentence in a pre-Bitcoin email from Satoshi to one of the early contributors to digital money, a developer named Wei Dai, highlights this (all mails from that period have been stored for posterity and are available on www.bitcoin.com): 'A purely peer-to-peer version of electronic cash would allow online payments to be sent directly from one party to another without the burdens of going through a financial institution...'

Notice the pejorative *'burdens'*. Subtlety not required.

So the privatization and ownership of money was the first and most visible target of the social freedoms that the Cypherpunks sought. The target was big, and the technology converged and then on 11th January 2009, ten Bitcoins were sent from Satoshi to cryptographer and email list member Hal Finney. And then, on 22nd May 2012, Florida-based programmer Laszlo Hanyecz managed to convince a nineteen-year-old Jeremy Sturdivant to accept 10,000 Bitcoin for two pizzas, giving the cryptocurrency its first commercially pegged value. $41.

And so it began.

* * *

Recapping what we have said before – cryptocurrencies are a specific kind of cryptotoken, meant to mimic, replace or improve upon real world 'money'. This includes being used as a medium of exchange or a store of value or, in some cases, a somewhat more exotic fungible financial asset. The world of cryptotokens is a superset of cryptocurrencies, and includes things like NFTs and governance tokens, which have somewhat different and broader use cases than cryptocurrencies. There is a reason we want to repeat this differentiation.

And that is because we suggest that the secure ownership of money has a very different emotional resonance than the ownership of, say, a book or a car or a jacket or passport. Money sits at the root, it is the base nutrient for the economic food chain. The loss of money is like our trapdoor function: it cannot be reversed. The loss of a book or a passport or art feels different, perhaps related to their non-fungibility, or replaceability. I suppose one could debate this differentiation endlessly on the head of the pin, but the fact that money represents the future ownership of arbitrary objects gives it a greater utility and fluidity and therefore makes it deserve a special kind of secure ownership.

Not only that. The ownership of 'objects' generally requires less privacy, in everyday life. We tend to keep our financial affairs more private, other than the boastful billionaire. Objects certainly give an indication of our wealth, but it is less tethered than the raw accounting of money, the source of the purchase.

But there is something more fundamental that gave the blockchain pioneers energetic grist for their cryptocurrency mill. It is this – money, created and distributed by government-authorized central banks and lent to commercial banks is *never* ours. It is always owned by the state. This makes the ownership proposition more powerful when applied to money than when applied to things that we actually can own. So this argument follows – I can, in principle, claim ownership of anything that is rightfully mine, like my computer, even if I am thwarted in that claim because it was stolen and it is on its way to an anonymous resale. In principle, it still belongs to me. But not money. Money is *always* on loan to me by my government. I do not even stop to consider an alternative. Which is, obviously, what if there was a way to actually own my own money?

A beguiling thought indeed, now made real.

But even if one accepts the arguments in favour of privately owned, non-debasable global digital money to replace the non-private loans we have been issued from not-always-trustworthy states, there is the pressing matter of scale. How do you get from a single ten-Bitcoin transfer in 2009 from Satoshi to Hal Finney to over a hundred million Bitcoin wallets at the time of writing this book, perhaps accelerating to billions?

This perhaps is the one riddle without a clear answer. From two users to 100 million in twelve years demands an explanation. One could be generous and assume that 100 million people immediately understood the ownership/privacy proposition and bought into the philosophy and understood the underlying technical mechanisms. But in my other life as a columnist and educator, I can pretty much guarantee that is not the case. The ruminations and economic musings that underpinned the original development of Bitcoin were exchanged amongst a small cadre of enthusiasts. I suggest that there is a very small percentage of Bitcoin holders who bought or use Bitcoin or any other cryptocurrency out of some combination of well-considered defence mechanism or protest or activism.

This leaves us with an uncomfortable alternative narrative. Which is that people buy Bitcoin with their entire hopes pinned on appreciation of price. Uncomfortable because at their core each Bitcoin purchase was made out of a soft greed. Consider a counterfactual – if the rise in the price of Bitcoin was held to some modest inflation index number by some hypothetical mechanism, the user base could not possibly have grown as fast.

But so what? One could look at Venezuela or Turkey, where inflation and state mismanagement have laid waste to the value of local currencies. Or Ukraine, where war has blown up security. The average citizen there who took the decision to exchange local currency for Bitcoin was not doing it in the expectation of making money (as an investor in the US or Korea may have done), they were doing it to simply hold on to purchasing power. In countries like those the use case is very clear. It is secure ownership of a form of money that it shielded from value collapse. Those Bitcoin holders from those countries are going to think twice before returning to fiat currency – once trust is broken there, it is unlikely to return. And then one merely has to look around and make a prediction as to how many people in the world are likely to face economic hardship under the jackboot of poor economic decisions or extraneous events like climate change.

They will eventually turn to cryptocurrencies too: it is just good financial sense, even if it is only stablecoin like Tether or USDC, locked as they are to the value of a dollar.

There is one last more politically fraught narrative that may cause a massive move to cryptocurrency, playing out now in real time, and it is the tectonic reorganization in global power alliances. Those forces allied against the US chafe at the dominance of the dollar. But many do not have the financial strength to avoid requirements of dollar-denominated payments, such as for oil. One can imagine backroom conversations in Moscow or New Delhi. If trades can be done in cryptocurrencies rather than dollars, quickly and without the friction of current foreign-exchange control, the loser will be US financial dominance. These sorts of global political pressures were probably not foreseen by the OGs, who were more focused on the individual, but may end up serving as unlikely bedfellows.

Chapter 12

DAOS – AN EXPRESSION OF COMMON OWNERSHIP AND PURPOSE

Our story about this bright new thread of blockchain and tokenomics must be fuelled, for the purposes of this narrative, by two seemingly unrelated historical events.

The first event took place in Rochdale, Lancashire, in northern England, in 1884. Rochdale was in the centre of the textile-producing part of the country, crowded with industrial mills in which weavers were forced to work long hours in terrible and unsafe conditions for exploitative pay. To add insult to industry, Rochdale was a company town – all services, stores, land, houses and other foundations of survival were owned by the mills, forcing poorly paid workers to essentially return their meagre salaries to the companies as they bought food, clothing, haberdashery, lodgings and the small items that pretended comfort.

A modest group of people (somewhere between twenty-eight and forty-six, depending on whose history you read) organized a small pushback. They had little leverage with respect to their jobs or working conditions. But they would be damned if they would pay the company for their material needs for their hardscrabble private lives as well.

So they formed a co-operative, evangelized those with similar complaints to their cause, and attracted the princely sum of twenty-eight pounds, enough to start a small independent general goods store. Modest at first, just a few staples like flour, but more expansive later. All profits were shared among contributors who brought the store to life.

I presume that the textile bosses could have found any manner of means to stamp them out, but they probably decided the effort was not worth the money, and so it thrived, and spawned copycats all over the country, who eventually amalgamated into an agglomeration of co-operatives, smartly named Co-operative Wholesale Society by 1872.

A democratic organization. Disparate people, some unknown to each other, but with similar goals (including a few who had grown up in the area but had moved to greener pastures). Shared profits. Flattened hierarchy. Answerable only to the combined voice of their members.

Not the first co-operative in history, but remarkable for its founding documents, which described in great detail how it was all going to run and under what circumstances, all of which was agreed to by the co-operative members. Which we now refer to as the rules of governance. The overarching principles were – open membership; democratic control; distributing profits to members in proportion to their spending; paying small amounts of interest on capital; political and religious neutrality; cash trading; no credit; promotion of education; and quality goods and services.

A history of what happened and how it all unfolded is captured in detail in a book called *The History of the Rochdale Pioneers* by George Jacob Holyoake, published in 1900.[28]

A couple of remarkable items jump out. The author's other two books are *A History of Co-operation in England* and *Sixty Years of an Agitator's Life*. The subtitle reads: *Self-Help by the People*. The dedication is to 'Lord Brougham, who never ceased to advance THE INTELLECTUAL AND SOCIAL WELFARE, and who lent, when no one else in his position would, the influence of his name, FOR THE PROMOTION OF SOCIAL SCIENCE of which co-operation is the industrial part'.

Caps and fancy old typefaces abound. This whole tenor of the first few pages pleased me, in a non-cynical sort of way. Here was empathy and community spirit digitized from yellowed old paper at the turn of the twentieth century, brimming with an early enthusiasm for tenets of socialism.

In other words, an organization of clearly defined common purpose, somewhat outside of the business norms and in resistance to the power structures of the time.

Hold that thought.

The next historical matter was a barely noticed affair that occurred in a surprising corner of the US, Wyoming, in 1977. Until that point the dominant fictional structure of business in the US was the corporation. There is a reason for the word 'fictional'. The corporation was and is, a story invented by humans to organize, govern and execute a plan towards a business goal.

There is a long and winding history here, stretching back, at least in the West, to around the time of the Dutch East India Company, which was 'chartered' by the government in the Netherlands in the 1600s, mainly to sell stock to fund important matters like ships and crew to go and get stuff like spices and silk in faroff places, often violently.

In fact, there are far earlier examples of this business construct, or reasonable facsimiles, dating back to the Romans and before, but this rabbit hole is long and convoluted, so before we get distracted…

By 1977 the structure of the corporation had become an ossified beast, with high walls of legal, statutory and administrative bricks to be scaled – articles of incorporation, board of directors rules, company officer requirements, shareholder agreements, banking mandates, signatures upon signatures and on and on. Not to mention onerous reporting expectations and, critically, a double-taxation requirement (one tax for the corporation itself, one for those shareholders receiving dividends from the corporation's successful labours). Anyone who has set up a corporation from scratch (I have) can attest. It is not fun. It sucks away time and occasionally your will to live. Or you can pay a lawyer king's ransoms to handle it for you.

So what happened in Wyoming? In that quiet corner of America the legislature sought to bring to life a simpler structure for conducting business, particularly with regards to liability, taxation and management. Liability was at the core – any legal landscape in which stakeholders could be legally responsible for the possibly malfeasant or negligent activities of the business was a hindrance to people looking to risk capital to start or grow businesses. Any company in which the scaffolds of management decision-making were as brittle as the corporation was similarly seen to be a drag on growth. And as for double taxation, well that was just offensive to the investment spirit. (It turns out that the search for limited liability has been around for a while – a famous 1831 US lawsuit regarding the ship *The Rebecca* centred around a winning argument that investors in the vessel were only liable for their investment, and nothing more, notwithstanding more expensive or injurious claims that may have accrued).

Wyoming's contribution was the limited liability company, known as an LLC, which was approved by the Wyoming legislature, and some years later was grumpily accepted by the IRS, but not without some toing and froing. These days, new LLCs outpace new corporations by four to one.

A sidebar – there seems to be something in the water in Wyoming, with all that open country and horses. It is the most crypto-friendly state in the country, and as a consequence has become home to a host of well-known crypto companies in the last few years. It is also the home of Caitlin Long, one of the true heroines of the crypto field, battling bravely against the forces of torpor and resistance in Washington.

Bringing these two historical events together and gluing it all together with blockchain and cryptotokens gives us the core principles of a DAO. A project of common purpose, wherein members (token holders) all have a stake and an influencing voice, strong protections against liability (with some caveats), and only a personal responsibility to declare taxes if appropriate.

Common ownership. Common influence. Common rights. Common purpose. Tilman's second category of ownership from Chapter 1.

Well, at least in theory, and perhaps, occasionally in practice. We'll get there...

Before we dive into the history of Decentralized Autonomous Organization and use cases and their impact on the concept of ownership, consider the 'organizing principle'. The history of human endeavour is suffused with the need to create groupings and collectives and to build governance structures around those organizations in order to keep them on their rails. Without which civilization would simply be a series of tiny individual goals and aspirations, without the multiplying power of community action (I do not mean to exclude the rest of the tree-of-life here – organization can be found in many species, but only humans have been able to codify and spread rules of organizational structure through language and writing).

From political systems to religions to educational institutions to business, and down all the way to micro-projects like organizing a picnic, we are awash in the minutiae of tasks and responsibilities and resource allocations and timelines and rules in pursuit of a larger goal. Furthermore, many of these structures are organized into centralized hierarchies, with key decision-makers at the top and unquestioned adherence to instructions and directives at the bottom. The typical triangle of management – one boss, a bunch of execs, many managers, and many more workers at the base.

In a perfect world this works well. Those higher up the triangle are there because of trust or skill or vision or equity ownership. Without them the entire enterprise flails. CEOs, presidents, headmasters, project managers, savvy administrators anywhere. But where there are humans there is sure to be error, failure, malfeasance, incompetence, cruelty. And often we see the centralized hierarchical organizations not only fail to perform their mission but also the damage and discomfort meted out to those lower down on the stack who find themselves without voice or influence and at the receiving end of all manner of nastiness.

And so we get tens of millions dead in Stalin's Russia or Mao's China, all the way down the chain to the picnic that was ruined because the organizer forgot the plates. Failures of centralized hierarchical organization – they are all over history. Of course, successes of centralized hierarchical organization – they are all over history too.

A final word about the history of governance. I had hoped to avoid this (because I am not a historian) but history is a guide to many things, so I have to talk about the *Federalist Papers*.

The American Constitution was drafted in Philadelphia in 1787. We know it now to be a work of great intellectual and philosophical gravitas (notwithstanding the ugliness and confusion around its intents now poisoning the American political landscape). It has been copied and admired for millennia. It has also been at the core of America's promise and dream. In 1787 it was discussed, argued, debated and panel-beaten by some of America's greatest minds, both political and philosophical. But the ratification of the final draft was by no means guaranteed.

And so a series of eighty-five essays appeared in New York newspapers written pseudonymously by great American politicians and philosophers James Madison, Alexander Hamilton and John Jay, all of whom had a hand in the drafting of the constitution and published under the moniker Philo-Publis. The essays had one goal – to convince people that the draft US Constitution was moral and practical, and to get behind it. History, clearly, was swayed in its favour.

Not having any scholarly expertise in this area, I am going to tread carefully, but there are certainly some matters of governance that bear directly on the subject at hand, DAOs. One matter was to explain the unratified Constitution's governance recommendations that sought to avoid the tyranny of the majority. Another was to propose democratic representation by delegates, who presumably had skills and knowledge not available to everyone. And another was to enforce the independence and non-collaboration of the great pillars of power – executive, legislature and judiciary. All of these goals have felt the warp of reality at various points of America's history, especially now. But they were and are laudable, and the maturation of DAOs bear no small resemblance to the matters debated 250 years ago. The most important aspect the *Federalist Papers* sought to convince people of was that the Constitution facilitated a *decentralization* of power where it believed it to be in the people's interests (the famed 'more perfect Union') – it was the framers' best expression of a perfect democracy.

In the world of technology, decentralized systems have a long and storied history, as soon as computer power started to move from monolithic mainframes to more distributed architectures in which there was no uber-computer orchestrating the show. The Internet protocol (IP) itself was an attempt to solve this problem, where any computer in a network could drop out without shutting down the others – the system could easily reroute itself autonomously.

Decentralization gathered steam in the 90s as the magic of the integrated circuit provided the ability to power 'edge' devices, somewhat smaller than the big central computer, but utterly capable of being computers themselves. Like your smartphone today. The massive central computers have retreated to custom applications and deployments (like the supercomputing beasts doing specialty tasks in subjects like particle physics). In the 90s computer architects and network designers started to come up with models that require no centre at all (remember Napster? Ever use BitTorrent?). To say nothing of IoT (Internet of Things) where thousands of little guys (like low-cost sensors) could cooperate, existing decentrally, reporting centrally.

But alas.

Up until blockchain, pure and unsullied decentralization, not only in tech, but in every other field of human enterprise, was a little illusory. They always seemed to be some level of structure that required a centre. Maybe the tech was dispersed, but there was a corporation or partnership or LLC controlling a bank account that wasn't, sort of thwarting the whole purpose. Or in the case of the Internet, a central backbone or three. Even in the world of blockchain there is accretion. A company called Infura wields enormous power in blockchain deployment (particularly Ethereum). If they went kaput, there would be trouble.

But why split hairs? Decentralization is an aspiration. And, I will argue, only worth its weight in selected circumstances, under constrained conditions. Centralized control is both appropriate and welcome in many examples of human, technological and industrial organization.

* * *

This was a long lead-up – Rochdale co-operative pioneers, the Wyoming invention of LLCs, the organizing principle, the *Federalist Papers*, technology decentralization. It is time to look at DAOs and how they started and what they have become in less than seven years since they became a thing.

The history of DAO started in 2016 when GenesisDAO, later known as The DAO, was formed by a couple of Ethereum developers in order to attract capital to use to fund new companies. A sort of blockchain-governed VC fund. It was astonishingly successful, raising $150 million in about a week. And then catastrophe struck; the smart contract had a bug, and about $50 million was drained out, and, well, it was not a great beginning for DAOs.

We jump to November 2021. At the risk of choosing an over-flogged and overused example, we need to talk about ConstitutionDAO, a pop-up DAO that sought to purchase one of thirteen original copies of the US constitution that had come up for sale. There were originally 500 copies, thirteen survive now, and one of these was up for sale, having been purchased by a private collector in 1997. It started off as a tweet from one Austin Cain on 11th November 2021, in which he wrote that he and a friend, Graham Novak, were of a mind to start a DAO to purchase the copy of the Constitution at a Sotheby's auction six days hence. 'We have 6 days to acquire $20 million to acquire the Constitution of the United States', said a tweet from Austin.

17,437 people stepped up. $47 million was raised in six days. They lost the bid to a billionaire named Ken Griffin.

There are many things to say about this, and many interesting details that I will jump over. The most important is this. What other mechanism would allow $47 million to be raised from 17,437 people in six days from conception to funds? Partnership? Corporation? LLC? Even one of the many online crowd-funders like Kickstarter? None. There was no chance that this could have happened without the DAO, whose treasury was lodged on the blockchain, and whose wallet address was publicly available, and that automatically emitted tokens called $PEOPLE to all 17,437 investors, which assured them of their ownership in the DAO. The DAO was built in hours, the word was spread on social media, and six days later they had the money. That is truly astonishing.

Through the lens of crypto-ownership this is what had been achieved – an organization of clearly stated common purpose, securely and impartially owned by the members who capitalized it, anonymity of contributors, unbounded by geography or legal constraint, permissionless, without a hierarchy of management.

But there were a couple of weaknesses, most likely borne out of haste. Firstly, they had no plans with what to do with the document if they had won the auction. Or what to do with the $PEOPLE token beyond the auction. And Sotheby's was not initially ready to accept ETH for the purchase (an exchange solution was designed and accepted). And the actual rules for bidding (and other governance matters) was not encoded in the ConstitutionDAO smart contract, and so it had at least one centralization point – a human bidder was assigned. And the return of the unspent funds to investors was debased by the high energy fees in Ethereum.

But it didn't matter. The publicity surrounding this opened the floodgates of DAOs that came afterwards, and fuelled a sudden interest from the media and public.

At the risk of redundancy, let's state the proposition again. Traditional means of governing organizations are fairly inflexible structures that define a set of rules that everyone agrees on. Many of these are standardized, such as in memoranda of agreement, shareholder agreements, charters. This is as true of corporations, as it is of the Girl Scouts, as it is of a city municipality. Implementation is handed off to hierarchies of human beings, who enforce those rules and make decisions in the service of the organizing principles, with greater or lesser efficacy.

The DAO works without humans. It encodes the rules of the organization in a smart contract, and invites DAO participants to join the DAO, safe in the knowledge that the rules cannot be flouted or bent. They are committed by the mathematics of cryptography and the execution of the smart contract. Moreover, no one needs permission, and DAO token holders have the right to both make proposals as to changes or upgrades or pivots or anything else, and obviously to vote on these proposals.

The matter of 'proposals' is sometimes fraught, with generally only a small percentage of DAO holders having the skill, time and motivation to make proposals, which can be basically anything. It has echoes of a legacy shareholder proxy statement, which is sent out to shareholders when the board wishes to make some substantive change. If you have ever seen a document you will know that they are often written in incomprehensible corporate and legal speak, leaving most shareholders to shrug and approve. DAO proposals, especially for large complex projects, are no better, often written in tech-speak which whizzes over the head of most token-holders.

In any event, the DAO industry has spawned a slew of easy-to-use toolsets – build-your-own-DAO apps, with drag-and-drop and checkboxes. Building a DAO is now as simple and permissionless as is joining one.

What could go wrong, right?

A number of things.

The most obvious one is that some organizations are just too complex to encode as a set of rules to be committed to

a smart contract. When one considers the number of decisions that need to be made by a skilled CEO or other senior
management every day, often in reaction to extraneous and
unpredictable events, it quickly becomes obvious that these
cannot be reduced to a set of IF-THEN statements. The real
world simply does not submit to that sort of reductionism.
The flexibility and fluidity of nuanced decision-making in
areas of great complexity requires the sort of intuitive thinking human beings do well. Hierarchies exist for a reason,
and that is because some people have expertise, and make
better decisions.

And so contrary to the zeal of some DAO maximalists,
the DAO is not going to entirely challenge the legacy of
regulated and human-run organizations soon. Even if we
reduce the applications of DAOs to scenarios with clear and
programmable objectives and a flat democratic structure,
other problems lurk.

Consider a DAO that seeks to attract capital to disburse to
charity. No management team is required, the rules encoded
in the smart contract take a vote from DAO members and
disburse to the top ten member-selected charities, perhaps
monthly. In order to join the DAO, one need only to buy
$CHARITY tokens, which are held in the member's wallet.
Now consider this scenario. There is one very rich philan-
thropist who wants the bulk of the DAO's contribution to
go to one charity, the board of which includes his wife. So
he simply buys up an outsize number of $CHARITY tokens
with his blockchain-guaranteed anonymity (or better still,
opens 1,000 different wallets each to buy a small amount of
tokens), and forces the previously democratic vote to favour
his chosen charity. Democracy be damned. It doesn't take

much imagination to see how this can be abused in circumstances where the stakes are less noble than charity.

This DAO vote-loading is a real phenomenon, widely reported, particularly where early investors end up with the bulk of the voting tokens, making DAOs look somewhat like the systems they were meant to replace. Of course there is fight-back, and new mechanisms constantly being trialled to prevent this abuse, but that fight will never end, particularly in DAOs where large numbers are at play, like Uniswap, a decentralized exchange. It is run as a DAO, with nearly $5 billion in total token value. One can imagine the incentive to own an influential stack of UNI, the DAO governance token.

And of course, there is the matter of regulation. DAO membership is somewhat like owning voting shares – it gives the owner a voice in directing the future of the DAO. What then of legal rights of the DAO token holder? If there is no legal entity, no CEO, no board, then who is to be held liable when it all goes pear-shaped (do not imagine for a moment that because a DAO is governed by a smart contract it can't go pear-shaped). So regulators have turned their attention here, perhaps less harshly than in other areas of crypto, with Wyoming, unsurprisingly, at the leading edge, becoming the first government in the world to pass a law allowing DAO members to defend voting rights, proposal outcomes and executed transactions in court. The first regulatory steps are small, like protecting developers from liabilities in the case of DAO liability. But there is still a way to go, the two most important being the recognition of a DAO-emitted token as something with a legal canon, perhaps a security, or even something new. The second is to move regulation from state to federal level – don't hold your breath.

Casting our gaze backwards at the representations of ownership we have already discussed – we have cryptotokens called NFTs that look a bit like title deeds to digital and physical stuff, we have cryptotokens that mimic money, like Bitcoin and other cryptocurrencies, and cryptotokens that look like yield-bearing financial instruments in Defi, and cryptotokens that look like voting shares in DAOs. It is worth noting this because ownership is a broad tent.

* * *

Hindrances and challenges aside, what is the state-of-play with DAOs now? As of mid-2023, there were over 12,000 DAOs in existence, according to the analytics firm DeepDAO.io. DAO token-holders number over seven million, and a total of over $28 billion sitting within DAO treasuries. Although this last metric, the treasury, is a little meaningless – many DAOs do not have financial motives at all – they are merely democratic non-hierarchical communities of interest run and guided by the wisdom of its crowd. Similarly, the number of DAO members is also not an important metric. Having more DAO token holders does not imply a better organization. Not all communities of interest require or even desire a large collective.

But for what it's worth: all of the largest DAOs sit in the Defi ecosystem. At the top of the pile is Uniswap, with nearly $4 billion its treasury and about 400,000 token-holders. Of that number only about 5% are active in governance – making and voting on proposals. This percentage is about average across the Defi DAOs.

But if you ignore the big money financial DAOs in this space, we get to what seems to me to be a more interesting group. Tokenhq.com presents a simple taxonomy:

- Social DAOs – promoting digital democracy though special interest networking and communication.
- Grant DAOs – disbursing funds to worthy public goods.
- Investment DAOs – investment club and venture capital.
- Media DAOs – connecting artists directly to fans and aligning incentives between them.
- CollectorDAOs – pooling funds to acquire art and other collectables (like ConstitutionDAO).
- Protocol DAOs – guiding blockchain technical strategies and tactics.

One of the more interesting DAO experiments bears mentioning. Its name is NounsDAO, and it started in late 2021. The protocol mints one NFT per day, a little blocky avatar that randomly mixes bodies, accessories, backgrounds, glasses and heads from an image library to produce a cute little character, never to be minted again. An auction is held, and anyone may buy the currently minted Nouns NFT. The funds from the auction go into a treasury. Nouns NFTs graphics can be repurposed without restriction to make other graphics by anyone. All Noun NFT holders have a voice in how the treasury should spend their money – proposals can be made on what to spend it on. Like aid for Ukraine, or starting a fashion brand, both of which were proposed and passed.

And every twenty-four hours another Noun is minted and actioned, adding funds to the treasury, which are then put to purpose by the DAO members. It is a strange virtuous circle, like a continuously replenishing venture capital fund.

They currently have about $50 million in the treasury, a recognizable brand, a 'club' and an active community deciding on how to spend the money that pours in daily, guided by immutable rules of governance. One wonders what equivalent could be imagined that could have achieved this in a pre-blockchain world.

We leave the world of DAOs by returning to our core thesis. This blockchain-secured structure of governance allows all stakeholders not only an ownership stake (like a share), but an ownership of the future of the community – an ability to propose new things, to vote. To inject your *identity* into the community in which in part belongs to you.

To have a voice.

Chapter 13

METAVERSE – THE WORLD BUILDERS

We start out with two problems here, at least. The first is a matter of definition. The second is a matter of believability.

My own very recent live poll, consisting of exactly two people close to me, both with master's degrees and impressive careers, was interesting. What's the metaverse? I asked one friend, who spends most of her days online, writing, reading and researching and occasionally messing around on social media. Hmm, she answered. A sort of 3D virtual world where you go to hang out and buy stuff? (Her voice lilted up at the end, like when you turn an answer into a question because you are unsure.) The second friend I asked is highly technology-literate. A bit of a polymath, actually. I asked him, do you think the metaverse will be a thing? He didn't. Emphatically. Why would anyone want to spend time there, he asked, incredulous.

So we jump into this chapter, and its connection to our ownership thesis suffering from both specificity and credulity problems. My first friend's definition turns out to be reasonable. My second friend's lack of faith turns out to be at odds with the smart money pouring into this space, although that slowed down significantly in the first quarter of 2003, but is poised to pick up again with the arrival of the big AI (ChatGPT and friends), which promises novel and ever-changing real-time environments. On the other hand, my second friend is mostly right about stuff, so I withhold judgement.

In any event let's race through the history of the metaverse, how it is different from its descendants and where it is headed, and (of course) how it lands on our ownership proposition.

At the end of October 2021, Facebook, one of the most famous brands on earth and one of the most profitable and influential companies in history, changed the name of its parent company from Facebook to Meta. Much derision was heard among tech wonks, and no small amount of concern amongst investors who rushed off to find out what it meant.

Mark Zuckerberg, in an internal memo to Facebook staff wrote: 'The defining quality of the metaverse will be a feeling of presence – like you are right there with another person or in another place. Feeling truly present with another person is the ultimate dream of social technology. That is why we are focused on building this.'

Early versions of the metaverse had been making themselves seen and heard for some time. The word itself was coined by sci-fi writer Neal Stephenson in his 1992 book *Snow Crash*.[29] The Internet was still a toddler, and Stephenson used it as a launchpad for his creative spark, imagining a completely virtual world in which we would live in some dystopian future. Given where we are now, and where we are headed, it seems uncannily accurate in some respects, although the dystopia part is a matter of fierce debate.

So when Mark Zuckerberg made the announcement he was describing something quite old. Second Life, an immersive online world released June 2003 by Linden Labs. It was a virtual world – you could assign yourself an avatar and go wandering around, watching your avatar's movement on the screen. You could meet other avatars and buy and sell land and build things.

It morphed into a sprawling social and land-based eco-system. This metaverse attracted one million citizens by the early 2010s. It was, by all measures, a success. It had moved from the early days of teleporting your avatar from one part of their geography to another, and morphed into events, gated communities, homeowners associations, land speculation and some darker behaviour, like sexual harass-ment. Denizens could trade virtual objects using internal currency called $LINDEN on a market owned and operated by Linden Labs. $LINDEN was exchangeable for $USD, but the process was economically opaque and definitely central-ized by the owners of Second Life. Second Life is still there, still has fans and regular players, but remains straitjacketed in its older architecture.

So when Facebook made their big announcement, it was a head-scratcher. This was not particularly new territory, and certainly not revolutionary. The metaverse was, in some circles, quite close to a cliche. And Second Life had launched nineteen years earlier, a lifetime in technology. Kara Swisher, podcaster and journalist, interviewed Neal Stephenson a few months later. Here is part of their exchange around the Meta announcement:

Stephenson: …it's hard for me to make out what they claim to be doing that's new, other than maybe implementing those old ideas on a larger scale for a broader audience.

Swisher: Yeah. It didn't feel very fresh in my estimation. Changing of outfits was also something I did, I don't know, ten years ago.

Not entirely fair, though. Because the announcement was backed up with the biggest of chequebooks, $10 billion investment to date, by some accounts, although now significantly curtailed. Facebook/Meta's imprimatur carried weight, and a ship of that size executing a pivot is sure to make waves. And a March 2022 Citibank research report[30] estimated that the metaverse economy could reach an addressable $13 *trillion* by 2030, serving 5 billion people. A recent McKinsey report forecasts that the metaverse will generate $5 trillion in revenue by 2030, more than the current size of the food or IT or automotive or oil and gas industries.

The metaverse, at least as discussed before and after this announcement, is not hard to grasp. We already spend a large part of our lives online. In my case about three hours per day on my iPhone, and about seven hours on my laptop (I was pretty shocked when I discovered this). Not in the metaverse of course, but on email and social media, writing, research, streaming. I live glued to my mobile and PC, but I don't consider myself to be living in a virtual world any more than I would have sixty years ago with a notebook, typewriter, rotary telephone, radio and TV set. They simply got combined into one or two devices, and I still talk to human beings within earshot even though my devices are on and connected and waiting on my attention.

But the metaverse is a much more intrusive view of the future. The cliche 'immersive' is bandied about a lot. As in 'sink'.

We will sink into an environment, 3D, perhaps augmented by headset, haptic and other-sense interactions and sort of live there a lot of the time. Interacting with other people's personal avatars, having AI pets, shopping, milling around, making stuff, sightseeing, flirting, marrying, learning, dancing, being entertained, trading, buying, selling. It is maybe instructive to consider what we *will not be able to do* in order to draw the walls around which an all-encompassing metaverse might envelop us.

Eating. Sleeping. No wait, I suppose sleeping can be augmented by devices – earphones, for instance. OK, sex. No wait, I can imagine scenarios where… forget it. Child rearing. Yes, one has to do that in the real world, but I suppose there are scenarios where… forget it. Exercise! No wait…

In the most extreme of dystopian imaginations, eating and bathroom activities may be about the only thing that one can think of that might escape the metaverse, and I am sure that there are those who could think up counterfactuals. But my personal gut horror at all of this is irrelevant, there are certainly those who see it leaning into utopia, perhaps those of a different generation. To this last point a McKinsey consumer study asked different age groups how many hours per day they expected to spend in the metaverse in five years. Baby boomers reckoned 1.8 hours. Gen-Z and millennial responders thought it would be 4.7 hours.

So let us grant then that the metaverse is going to expand aggressively and possibly chaotically. Many 3D environments will be built, people will come and visit, perhaps stay, perhaps move on. Graphics will get better, perhaps even photorealistic as CPUs and software become more powerful.

How then is this different from an upgrade to Second Life? The answer is cryptographically secured property rights and cryptocurrency. There are other differences which I will come back to, but this is the core.

I am going to mention a few of the bigger and more successful metaverses later in the chapter but for the moment, I will build a hypothetical one, which is somewhat of a mishmash of whatever is out there now.

A cataclysmic volcanic eruption has caused a geological ruction on the seafloor. When the eruption has calmed, a new island has revealed itself in the middle of the Pacific. Being outside of anyone's territorial waters, it does not belong to any country. Moreover, the island is dotted with exotic long-sunk features of a previous civilization – an amphitheatre, tunnels, partially destroyed dwellings, strange devices, headstones and other mysterious structures, even life forms and flora never before seen. It seems like there may once have been an alien race living there (OK, I'll stop here, but you get the gist).

The island's name is Pacifi. Visitors are encouraged to visit and if they like it, to take out Pacifi passports. These are non-fungible NFTs, cryptographically tethered to the citizen. Each new citizen is awarded 100 PaCoins, to spend as they please, as they go sightseeing in the island, spend their PaCoins on entrance to exotic sites and buy souvenirs. PaCoins are fungible and trade on a public blockchain, so citizens can easily buy and sell them at market prices and exchange them for other cryptocurrencies.

OK, so no big deal so far, other than the fact that we now have non-fungible tokens (NFTs bound to passports) and fungible tokens (cryptocurrencies called PaCoins) in the same environment. How then do we get a virtual world that is not and does not become yawningly boring after a few visits? The answer is to offer the means to allow citizens to socialize, to organize events, to allow them to build structures and other items, to create art, to secure them with unforgeable property rights, and to create wealth if they so choose.

So Pacifi offers:

- A 3D modeller for structure and homeware building – either renovating water-damaged and half dissolved alien structures or building new ones and the interior contents. Each building or item can be owned via an NFT called PaBuild, which is a title deed, transferable and saleable using PaCoins.
- A 3D pet builder, allowing citizens to construct bizarre articulated pets called PaPets that ambulate or fly or roll or jump. They are owned via NFT.
- A 3D vehicle builder, allowing citizens to specify all manner of rolling or flying or sailing NFT-titled vehicles called PaCars, secured by a NFT PaCar registration.
- A market is provided for barter and exchange of NFTs or for direct peer-to-peer sales using PaCoins. NFTs can also be listed on external markets.
- The amphitheatre can be booked and performances given by citizens who can play the music they have created.
- Citizens can buy and rent fashion outfits using PaCoins, or borrow from the costume closet. Fashion shows with PaCoin awards are held.
- Land can be bought, sold, divided.
- Games can be designed by using a 3D game design tool that is provided by Pacifi. Games can be owned and titled by NFTs, and entry can be charged in PaCoins.

- Real life companies can be offered branding rights – for buildings, for fashion outfits, for vehicles, for streaming movies. Paid for in PaCoin.
- A simple tool is provided to form DAOs, communities of common interest, with their own rules and tokens of governance.

This is a somewhat haphazard and superficial list of what may be on offer on Pacifi island. But here's the rub. All of the features mentioned all exist in more sophisticated instantiations in existing metaverses like Decentraland and Sandbox and others, which support economies mixing NFTs and cryptocurrencies whose trading volumes are in the hundreds of millions of dollars since their inception. Real-world brands like Gucci and Adidas and others have rented spaces, and do real sales of their physical products through their retail shops in the environment. Avatars can meet and talk to other avatars, and exchange real-life connection details, piercing the virtual/physical wall. APIs allow developers to add VR helmet experiences like head-turning and even running (although an expensive harness device is required for this; there are videos on YouTube which made me giggle).

How real does this get? In 2022 a piece of land was purchased for $2.4 million in the fashion district in Decentraland. 800,000 people have registered profiles. Small plots in outlying areas cost about $5,000, but who knows, someone may build a school nearby with real-life celebrity teachers offering video tutorials, increasing land values. Someone could build a supertrain to a sparsely inhabited end of the island – remember what happened in the real world when a train line was built between LA and Salt

Lake City in 1905, and which stopped at a small outpost called Las Vegas.

The vision extends beyond here. Different metaverses will be connected via blockchain bridges, much in the same way that is happening elsewhere in the crypto world. 'Passports' could be accepted between different metaverses. Inter-metaverse currencies recognized. NFT-tethered 3D objects being made portable between one environment and another. To this last point, interoperability between anything in tech requires standardization, and so the Metaverse Standards Forum was promulgated in June 2022, whose membership reads like a who's who of technological influence, with over 1,500 organizations joining.

Entire worlds – social, economic, political, cultural, philosophical, educational, financial and connected to our physical world via headsets and electronic gloves and bodysuits and who-knows-what-else, splitting our identities down the fault line of digital vs corporeal. It is an enormous vision, this metaverse future which invites scepticism and disbelief on one side and breathless overreach on the other. So many technical hurdles to be overcome, so much to be questioned about our desire to spend time there and how real it is. Which brings to mind a quote from entrepreneur Shan Puri, who commented that the metaverse not a place but a time – the moment when 'our digital life is worth more to us than our physical life'.

There are so many lenses through which to view this new arrival in our digital futures. I suppose the one that cannot be overlooked is how much money is pouring into this space from investors and companies whose job it is to spot trends. At the top rung of this space there are those who saw the future of the transistor, PC, Internet, smartphone, greentech, healthtech, edutech and other constants in our lives before anyone else, and who staked money or time or effort with the confidence of the mad seer. According to McKinsey, in 2021 $57 billion was invested into the metaverse. That figure more than doubled by July 2022 – $120 billion. While that number is startling, it is not all into 'immersive environments'. It includes infrastructure and VR and AR and related technologies all contributing to the larger vision. But still, $120 billion! Although this is certainly somewhat tempered by investors turning away from metaverse and towards AI in 2023. Risk capital is nothing if not fickle.

Then there is a question of what, exactly, qualifies as a metaverse. Is it an all-encompassing 3D world, a place to hang out, socialize and have fun and build and create wealth? If so, is an 'immersive' videogame, where the goal is to kill enemies rather than just hang out a metaverse? And what of metaverse videoconferencing applications, as was demonstrated by Facebook some years back, where all the participants around the table were an avatar? Does that have enough oomph to qualify as a metaverse? And is a 'definition' really necessary, and who would benefit from it?

An article written by Eze Vidra, a partner at VC fund Reimagine Ventures on the website VCCafe, has a useful descriptor. He says, 'The term metaverse doesn't describe one specific technology, but rather the way we interact with technology.'[31]

I rather like this definition. It describes not a place, but a mode of interacting. But there is a missing piece here, because it is actually not 'us' interacting, but a closely tethered 'digital twin' who heads off into a world that we cannot bodily inhabit and does our bidding within that world.

If one is looking for economy of words I like this, from Jonathan Lai of the VC company Andreessen Horowitz: '…a virtual space with its own economy and identity system'.

This last definition, which includes the word 'identity', hits the mark. Once we can assign identities to citizens, players, objects and experiences via the cryptographic certainties of NFTs we are then in the terrain of enforceable property rights. Imagine Pacifi, where every object in the virtual world, from avatar to building to pet to vehicle to art to event tickets to localised voting rights lives within an NFT-ecosystem, even for those items not yet owned (or assigned), like common resources (plants, unincorporated land, the life forms that wander the island). Imagine further that these NFTs can be swapped, traded or held. And that new owners can alter the underlying object if they please, like reupholstering a piece of furniture in a dwelling.

Is it fair to say that in such an environment we will find ownership more secure and defined than we do in the real world in which we live? Certainly we will find objects that don't exist in the real world which we may wish to own (or build). We will also certainly find experiences that have no equivalent in the real world. And if there is a dispute (for example if we pay for an experience with PaCoins, a trip to an underground alien's lair or some such, and find it suboptimal), to whom do we appeal? Does the community elect a council of 'elders' to mediate, perhaps via PaVote governance tokens?

The entertainment value of metaverses is fairly easy to imagine; that is what Second Life was, at least originally. But as the virtual community grows, and both virtual and real-world commerce embeds, and communities of interest spring up via DAOs, the boundaries of this new world will expand well beyond mere entertainment. Add to this the concept of micro-metaverses – hospitals, universities, even political system experiments (anarchy or benign dictatorship for instance) and we have an intriguing narrative that begins to take shape.

It is this. We live in a physical world of identity and ownership and commerce, among other things. With the arrival of metaverses we are constructing a parallel virtual world of digital identity and ownership and money (among other things too). The wall between these two worlds is porous, because NFTs and cryptocurrency travel. Is it possible that metaverse societies could feed back their experiences, both good and bad, into the real world? Are we constructing a simulation which becomes the most effective training ground for our real lives?

Or, if you are of a dystopian view, perhaps the other way around.

* * *

I have talked about the two major differentiators between post-blockchain metaverses like Decentraland and pre-blockchain virtual worlds like Second Life – specifically integrated NFT-based property rights and cryptocurrency. But there are other differentiators, as outlined in a paper from the VC company a16z. Some of these are worth mentioning – metaverses are built from open-source code; owned by their communities; have their transactional data open for inspection; facilitate permissionless access; allow the community to direct future growth of the world. Pre-blockchain virtual worlds could not provide this set of features, at least not easily.

Herman Narula is an Indian-born tech entrepreneur, Cambridge-educated programmer and author of *Virtual Society: The Metaverse and the New Frontiers of Human Experience*,[32] which is often quoted on the future of the metaverse. When he speaks about it, as he often does in podcasts and interviews, his enthusiasm is infectious, often straying into history, philosophy and psychology. He argues that humans have always sought virtual worlds – from the Pyramids as an environment for the afterlife to fantasy football leagues. His definition of the metaverse is broad:

A network of meaningful objects – characters, events – that especially permeates real-world systems of meaning like music, culture, fashion and so on... this is a way of supercharging our culture. This is a way of giving people more ways of experiencing and connecting with the most important communities and people that they already value.

Of course he talks about ownership and tradeability, but goes a couple of steps further, arguing that 'metaverse' will really hit its stride when two things occur. The first is for the metaverse to really, truly be able to process thousands of participants at the same time. Like at a football match – every individual yell, scream and moan audio processed into a single audio environment, like in the real world. The second is to have every participant, into the tens of thousands, visible and individually pro-cessed and interacting onscreen, just like, for instance, at a real concert. If the technical architecture can handle this (which current metaverses cannot), it would raise the 'experience' to a new plateau. He has now made a step towards this via his company Improbable, which released a Beta version of the metaworld 'Otherside'. I watched a video of it, without actually being in the world, and it was indeed mesmerizing to watch and hear 4,500 participants interacting. Narula muses that if one could scale this up to 100 million or 1 billion people, you would have not a metaverse, but a country.

His second requirement for mass traction would be the ability to take owned digital assets (like objects or even identity) from one metaverse to another, in order to exist in sort of a 'multi-metaverse'. This is where his vision breaks from current videogames and corporate-designed metaverses, whose business models could never allow for their participants moving to other environments. This is demonstrated by Yuga Labs having co-operated and made their Bored Ape NFTs available to entertain the crowds in Otherside. Which is why Narula comments matter-of-factly that the new metaverse will be built on the bones of Web 2 attempts to control it.

* * *

Finally, I wanted to list the top ten metaverses (we have already mentioned Decentraland and Sandbox), but the fluidity and chaotic growth of the sector make this a fool's errand, at least given the schedules of publishing. But in looking at genres we can quickly spot 'flavours' of metaverse – all appealing to different sectors of the public – metaverses that alternatively favour social engagement, spatial exploration, gaming, NFT-building, environment-based VR usage, events and music environments.

This is exploration time, perhaps even pre-Cambrian, with the big breakouts still to come. Neal Stephenson's fiction and Second Life cracked the door open, and eventually crypto and the blockchain walked through it.

Chapter 14

GAMEFI – PLAYING FOR MONEY

Once upon a time, in the deep mists of history, I was a game developer. I lived in LA, had a freshly minted graduate degree in computer science from UCLA, and I landed a job developing games for a company that was in the toy business and had started a new division to catch the videogame wave.

I had no particular background in videogames or game design, I was not even particularly interested in playing them, but I liked the tech and the odd and eccentric sorts that were attracted to it. Dating myself somewhat, this was in the days before tooling – one was confronted by a games console from a big manufacturer and some minimal bootstrapping and development software. My job was to wrestle the hardware and internal software to the ground so that I could make pixels move around on screen. It was enormous fun.

So young was the industry at the time that each company that released a games console jealously guarded its secrets and, in some cases, sought to even discourage external developers from creating games for the console. Attempts to contact the console manufacturer to get questions answered about nuances of the chips or software often went deafeningly unanswered.

It was a horror of centralized control. It didn't last long. As soon as the console manufacturers realized the advantage of having independent game developers, they opened their gates, but not without a gatekeeper extracting fees for distribution and marketing and whatever else they could (like the sticker price for players who purchased the game).

The games market had moved from a zero start with Pong in 1972 to a $180 billion industry today – larger than the film and radio market combined. Along the way the industry learned to attract outside talent like developers and game designers and celebs and partnerships with other media, like film companies. They even learned to allow players to participate in in-game economies, as long as all trade was funnelled through corporate-owned markets.

And then blockchain arrived and cryptocurrencies and NFTs and, unsurprisingly, a fissure opened that quickly turned into an abyss.

On the one side there were game players who wanted nothing to do with cryptocurrencies or NFTs, and were very happy with the status quo of big-budget releases and their entry prices, and on the other side those upstarts (amusing to be called an upstart, given the demographic of traditional gamers) who wanted games to be community-owned, community-led, permissionless and driven by open fungible and non-fungible cryptotoken economies.

The first (very) public skirmish broke out with the release of a game called *Axie Infinity* in 2018 by a Vietnamese video game studio called Sky Mavis. This game was loosely modelled on *Pokemon*, which started as a card game in 1996 and became wildly popular in various formats over a long period, ranging from cards to anime to videogames to films to merchandise.

But *Axie Infinity* included startlingly innovative new tricks. It incorporated some of the first NFTs. These blockchain-borne certificates of ownership allowed players to 'mint' their own pets – cute little oval creatures which could then be put into battle or bred with other pets to make new cute pets.

This immediately created an in-game economy – these NFTs were instantly tradable via external blockchain markets, allowing players to buy and sell their pets using cryptocurrency.

Previous videogames had various mechanisms to buy and sell treasures or weapons, but this was the first successful blockchain-tethered game – gameplay and cryptocurrencies and NFTs and blockchains all rolled into one ecosystem. It became a huge success.

And this spawned a weird, real-world economy, mainly in the Philippines (for reasons that are a little unclear, but not really central to the story). At one point, nearly three million people were playing daily.

Once people realized that they could win battles, facilitate cute pet breeding and then mint the NFT of the new baby and sell it on an NFT market in return for cryptocurrency, all hell broke loose. I would ask you to reread the last sentence, but I'll just say it differently:

- Bayano, an unemployed twenty-something Filipino, logs on to *Axie Infinity*.
- He acquires an Axie pet (never mind the details glossed over here).

- He manages, via skilful gameplay, to get his Axie pet to breed...
- ...giving him another pet, his second. With its own NFT.
- He sells the NFT for his second Axie pet on a public Axie NFT marketplace, where cryptocurrencies can be used to trade the NFTs.
- He sells his cryptocurrency for real dollars on his local cryptocurrency exchange.
- He feeds his real family with his real dollars, which purchase real food at his local supermarket.

This is what is called 'play-to-earn'. Bayano, unemployed, can now feed his family by playing a video game. And now it gets weirder.

It costs money to start playing *Axie Infinity* (an entrance fee of sorts), after which you can start battling and breeding NFTs/pets. So a bunch of smart operators (including the giant venture capital company, Andreessen Horowitz) thought, wait a minute! If we stake a bunch of unemployed people to enter *Axie Infinity* and breed NFTs all day and then sell them on the Axie NFT marketplace and we share revenue with them then... we get rich and they feed their families. (The stakers grandly called themselves 'guilds'; staked players are called 'scholars').

Win-win, right? Well, yes, as long as the market for Axie NFTs is robust, going up, liquid, etc.

Lots of players with time on their hands – almost exclusively in developing countries – staked to play a game, sharing their NFT sales. Hundreds of thousands of players making a modest living by playing a video game, sometimes up to sixteen hours or more a day.

What could possibly go wrong?

What went wrong was that in 2022 a bunch of North Korean hackers managed to steal $600 million from the Axie ecosystem. I wrote an article on this at the time, confidently predicting the end of *Axie Infinity*.

I was wrong. *Axie Infinity* seems to have risen from the dead.

The reactions to play-to-earn were extreme then, and continue to echo now. The one set of objections was about the nature of the business model for the now vibrant play-to-earn market. It seemed a little, well, distasteful to have unemployed and sometimes desperate people working as hired gamers, sharing modest earnings with richer stakers. Felt like slavery of a sorts, although no one was forced to play, and many people did in fact keep poverty from their doors for a period.

It also felt wrong to have a real dollar economy built around what some people think is a superficial and trivial activity like breeding or shooting things. I do not agree. People make things and buy things and sell things. That's how the world works. No one is forcing the play-to-earn commerce to operate at gunpoint; whether someone thinks this is a waste of human capital exists as an opinion only, at least until someone offers an alternative to the player/earner.

There continue to be strong opinions within the gaming community as to the gaming purity or lack thereof that will result from community ownership, blockchain-based property rights, NFTs and cryptocurrencies. But the cat is out of the bag now, and all indicators are that this new style of gaming will become dominant, even in the face of some big gaming companies swearing that they will resist. Among these is Valve, a videogame company and distribution platform representing 3,400 games and servicing 150 million players.

In the past, videogames were played for fun, for the joy of winning or just getting better. Then companies started to post names (or pseudonyms) of top players. Then hosting videogame extravaganzas and making celebs out of the best players – sponsorship, prizes, fan clubs. But that hierarchy of skill didn't really affect the average player. Fun and skills acquisition and winning still ruled the roost of emotional current. Until blockchain, where a new economic system suddenly appeared:

You can get better at it, you can have fun, you can win and… you can build stuff, own stuff, win stuff and make money. Anonymously, if you choose.

That's a whole different level of economic incentive.

And so I will hazard that the old innocent style of play will play second fiddle to play-to-earn, excuse the pun. There will continue to be games with corporate-controlled economies, and games without any property rights and trading component at all. But my gut tells me that blockchain-supported games will become dominant. And play-to-earn is soon to morph into something else.

Which brings me to Bronwyn Williams. Bronwyn is a futurist, author, columnist, podcaster, economist, among other things. But that's not the impressive thing about her. She once proclaimed on Twitter, without false modesty, 'Give me a topic, and I will give an unprepared talk on it, for thirty minutes.' Or something close to that. She can, and does. Now that's impressive. In any event, the reason I introduce her here is that she is a partner in a company called Metanomic.

Metanomic launched early in 2021. Their big idea? The pieces of software under the rubric of 'videogames' are basically gamifications of their economics systems – a series of incentives for players to make decisions around scarcity, which is the core of economic systems. Yeah, the games were fun and all, but the ownership and trading component meant that without a solid underlying economy, the games would be unsustainable. In my brief experience as a game designer and developer (I have three or four under my belt, depending on how one counts), there has been very little crossover between economists and the games world.

This is the gap into which Metanomic has stepped. Take some economists, AI-heads, game developers and software nerds and throw them into a pot and this is what came out. A company providing services to the game industry to allow them to balance, simulate, optimize and finetune their economies for player retention and to study player classification and behaviour, a feedback loop for refinement and improvement.

Bronwyn relates the genesis of the company. In April 2021 she teamed up with another futurist, Theo Priestly to write a book called *The Future Starts Now: Expert Insights into the Future of Business, Technology and Society*[33]. In the course of their collaboration, Priestly expressed his desire to design and build a videogame, but he had never done so before and wasn't sure where to start. I am amused by this story – it sounds a little like a teenager's secret dream which had been struggling to get out for too long, and their partnership gave it oxygen.

And so the seed of an idea was formed and it was to be their game's differentiator – this was going to be the first game built on firm economic principles. So they turned to academia to find out whether there has been any serious work done on the economics of videogames. And they came upon one Edward 'Ted' Castronova, a professor of media at Indiana University Bloomington. He had written extensively on the subject, including a book written well before crypto – the 2006 title called *Synthetic Worlds: The Business and Culture of Online Games*[34]. Castronova has been thinking about game and economics for a long time, and Bronwyn and Theo gladly hitched a ride on his analysis.

All of this was meant to build a foundation for the game idea that they had hatched. But it didn't take long for them to realize that there may be a bigger market for their economic software than for the game itself, and hence Metanomic.

Here is how it works. Most traditional Web2 videogames do not have the sort of blockchain-secured ownership, tradable property rights and cryptocurrency portals that we have talked so much about. They are fantasies, from top to bottom. They do not have to submit to the dictates of real world economic sustainability.

The new crop of blockchain play-to-earn games like Axie have certainly been a new wrinkle in the game landscape, but they suffer from a painful Achilles heel. They are, as Bronwyn points out, a multi-level marketing scheme. You need new players to come and trade at higher prices, or else the whole economy comes tumbling down. Players lose interest quickly if their pet or sword or shield is losing value in public markets. The economics of play-to-earn is not infinitely sustainable, it is guaranteed to lose its energy and deflate at some point.

Bronwyn and Theo's big idea? Not play-to-earn. But rather play-*and*-earn. Underpinning this are the imperatives of economic incentive. If everyone in a closed system has an identical incentive, paralysis and crash awaits. If stakeholders have different incentives, and balance between those incentives can be maintained, then sustainability is achievable. This is how real markets work. Buyers and sellers. One person wants money, the other wants the utility of the thing they bought. You are a car salesman, you want your commission. I am the buyer, I want transport. Different incentives, fair trade.

And so they have sought to build an engine that constantly balances two sorts of players – one who is in it for money, and the other who is in it for pleasure. Keep them equally weighted and you have an economy. Matching the extrinsic (money) with the intrinsic (play). Or as Bronwyn wryly points out – it should behave like life – work *and* play.

The Metanomic product is still embryonic, but it seems to me to be an approach that is uniquely enabled by crypto-ownership. The incentives of a game can now be broadened and weaved into a more colourful tapestry. The economy can maintain vibrancy. And game designers using these tools can make a home for a diverse population of players for longer periods than either fantasy or play-to-earn games can do.

Gamefi, as the reader may have noticed, is simply a corner of the metaverse, which we have already visited. But it occupies a different texture – something that started as basically a distraction in a bar. The first Pong machine, which launched the late great Atari, indeed found its first home in a drinking establishment in Silicon Valley, something to keep punters occupied while they drank. It broke on the first day. When it was sent back for repairs it was found that it was not a computer problem – the coin container had overflowed. Videogames have made the trek from unadulterated escapist fun to serious economies with ownership security, while most of the rest of the metaverse have arrived at economic systems via other paths.

Metanomic, who saw this gap, will most certainly find a way to apply its learnings to the rest of the metaverse. If they gamify economics, there seems to be no end to where it can go.

Chapter 15

WEB3 – A NEW ARCHITECTURE, WITH A SMIDGEON OF DOUBT

Just about everything we have discussed coalesces here. The Internet. Or, more specifically the Web, which sits on top of the Internet and allows us to do stuff. The Web is our entry point and library-in-the-cloud, and the Internet is the network that zips bits around at our behest.

As you have no doubt noticed, I am an enthusiast about the portents of all this new technology. Particularly with regards to the re-engineering of ownership, our core thesis. But the red flag of scepticism distracts me now and again. Not so much to do with challenges of regulation and law, or the scams that will get perpetrated along the way, or the black swan bugs that will certainly appear. Something much bigger than that gives me pause.

So let's take a look at Web3, where it came from, what it is, what is promised, and I will save my raised eyebrows for later.

Most people do not even know or care that we are now in the era of Web2. Or that there even was a Web1 and what it looked like. And now this. Web3. Real soon now.

But the discussions of the so-called Web3 have got very ugly recently, with one side lining up to praise its promise as a beacon of virtue which will spread joy and goodwill to all humankind, and the other side lining up to declaim it as the devil's work, which will make the rich richer, the poor poorer, and the rest of us slaves.

Web1 (the original World Wide Web) was in the dark ages, the 1990s. It was mostly a one-way conversation. You clicked on a website, were fed images, text and sound, and were sometimes able to click on a link to take you elsewhere. Sometimes you could fill in a form and send it back. It was a simple machine, very useful for finding stuff and making some modest contact with the website to send them some data, like your contact details.

Web2 (or Web 2.0), which dominates where we are now, was born on the rising seas of increasingly sophisticated interactive capability and speed. Massive back-end databases, video, audio, artificial intelligence and all manner of fancy back and forths between you and the application. WhatsApp and Instagram and eBay and Uber and Airbnb. All Web2. Two-way conversations between you and a digital universe. And with the capability of the web user to be a producer of information as well as a consumer (think uploading a TikTok video or a photo of your cat to Twitter).

And then came crypto.

In 2014, a renowned crypto computer scientist, Dr Gavin Wood, who was then working on what is now the second largest blockchain, Ethereum, coined the phrase Web3. It was going to be like Web 2.0, only better. Fairer. Smarter. Democratized. And lots of adjectives like that. Because, well, the blockchain.

What he was reacting to was the increasing centralization of the Web into the hands of large and dominant power centres

– Facebook, Amazon, Netflix, Google, TikTok, Alibaba, Microsoft and others.

The Internet had originally been a project to evenly spread the global accessibility of information (remember the quaint 'information wants to be free'?) and had tragically turned into the march of the elephants, with massive streams of capital rerouted from other places into a few companies, many of them now largely competition-proof.

The internet had turned from a democracy into a council of autocrats.

Woods and others realized that the sort of cryptographic magic embedded in blockchain technology could provide the tools to build a decentralized Internet and Web, owned by its users, with no middlemen extracting usurious rent and forcing on us their preferred content.

Well, yes, that sounded very nice. Still does.

Here is the way it is supposed to work:

The vision of Web3 is that the people who use the web will own it and will be incentivized and motivated to build it and direct it. Not a few huge companies. Users only. That's basically it.

Everyone on Web3 will have property rights, protecting their own data (all data, including how you traverse the Internet). Your own data would be kept private at your election, or potentially traded on markets, priced at fair value for you and the buyer.

Not only data about you, of course, but data *by* you – like your blog and posts and comments and your cat videos. Or even your attendance at a webinar. Or your identity. All may have value to you (or someone else) – but it is yours first. And will be owned, kept private, sold or ceded under the Web3 user's option. As a subset of this, of course, is cryptocurrencies, baked into the fabric of Web3 – the lubricant that will seamlessly integrate into all of this to allow exchange of value.

It is not only the end-user and her data that Web3 proponents want to protect. It is the infrastructure too. No owners, no middlemen, no choke points, no censors, no exploitation, no shareholder influence, and if one follows this to its logical conclusion, no 'companies' in the traditional sense, just communities-of-interest. And critically, community *governance* of the next Internet – the users get to shape it as they see fit. Secured and hardened by the magic of the blockchain.

The devil is in the details, but you get the drift. A huge vision. Alarmingly complex sets of technologies and economics and processes need to be invented to make it all happen. Many of the pieces are already under way, like cryptocurrencies and NFTs and DAOs. And the smartest programmers and computer scientists lining up to contribute and build the rest.

So, at the risk of oversimplifying – Web1 = read. Web2 = read & write. Web3 = read & write & own.

Yes, well. Now let me introduce you to some sceptics.

Molly White is a twenty-eight-year-old who lives with her pets in Massachusetts. She is of the Internet generation and spent a long stint as a self-admitted contributor-obsessive on Wikipedia. She has also created the website web3isgoinggreat.com.[35] It is a compendium of Web3 scepticism, including her own blog. She has become somewhat of a star in this world.

A recent *Washington Post* article on her makes her case – Web3 is 'filled with a litany of scams, failures and frauds meant to separate regular people from their money'. A careful read of the malcontent links on her website reveals the documenting and decrying of the many, many scams all over cryptocurrencies and the NFT world. Which of course is true, but I would argue that this is early-day opportunistic malfeasance as opposed to a foundational problem.

More convincing is Moxie Marlinspike, the creator of the Signal messaging app, who argues that some systems naturally tend towards centralization, and to equate this sort of accretion with evil and oppression is a bit silly. He wrote a 4,000-word essay[36] to make this and other arguments against Web3 evangelism.

His missive dived deep, and sparked some discomfort for me. Marlinspike is a technologist, and his worries are deep in the weeds of the architecture of computer science. I am going to try and describe it because it is important. In the Web2 world in which we live, when you open your mobile and click on an icon representing an application like Uber, your phone connects to a very powerful computer in a data centre somewhere in the world, using the mobile network and then a bunch of cables running underground and undersea to get there. The computer in the data centre does all the heavy lifting. It routes your pick up and destination address to a driver, who also has their mobile connected to it, and it downloads routes and time estimates and payment info and all the rest of the process. The computer in the data centre is doing this for thousands of riders and drivers simultaneously. It is a big job. It needs a big, fast, powerful machine (or collection of machines) to handle all of it.

It is called a server. And the mobile in your hand is called a client. And the whole Web2 ecosystem is built on these sorts of client-server architectures (or browser-server architectures, much the same thing). Big uber-controlled mother machine in an air-conditioned warehouse somewhere and a small not-so-powerful machine with the end user. The whole experience is an orchestrated toing and froing between client and server.

And here is the big nasty truth about Web3 pointed out by Marlinspike. The argument unfolds like this: users do not want to run servers. Not even technologically sophisticated users. It is complicated and gnarly – they have to be up 24/7 and are expensive and generate heat and use a lot of electricity and so on. So as much as we like to talk about a 'decentralized' Internet, it is never going to be fully that. There will always be client-server architectures because users want it that way; it is simpler to let someone else deal with the server wrangling. It will only be decentralized to the extent to which we can incentivize a very motivated but limited bunch of people to run complicated servers on our behalf. This is exactly how Bitcoin and Ethereum work – the 'nodes' and 'validators' we have talked about are running servers. When there are many distributed servers it is sometimes more accurately called a client-network architecture.

But it gets even worse. If there are going to be (in the fond imaginings of Web3 enthusiasts), a couple of billion Web3 users and perhaps a couple of thousand or even a couple of hundreds of thousands people hosting decentralized servers on their behalf, then how are all of those billions of people going to access the servers in order to make use of their new people-owned decentralized ride-hailing or shopping or messaging service?

One answer lies in another type of software called an API (application programming interface). This is like a 'gate' that allows outside clients to access servers. And guess what? This is most efficiently served by having a 'traffic cop' mediating all the requests for servers coming in from clients so that requests for service are delivered through the gateway in orderly fashion.

And that traffic cop works best when it is... centralized.

In the world of blockchain there are a tiny handful of these traffic cops, like the company Infura, who funnel client requests into the Ethereum blockchain and who hold massive power in the blockchain space. There are, of course, a number of new architectures getting batted around (including by Infura themselves) about how to decentralize their services. But that is by the by.

Here is the big takeaway. A completely 'decentralized' Internet or Web3 may not be achievable in any way that could be considered efficient or completely democratized. In fact the entire love affair with decentralization might be not only impossible to execute in full, but may also be partially counterproductive. Because the simple truth is that some things *tend towards centralization* – in technology, commerce, economy, society and politics. Sometimes hierarchies work, sometimes flat democracies don't, and it is the balance between them that becomes the open research question.

And so I claim that a vision of an Internet and Web utopia owned by its users and run autonomously is hope and optimism in extremis, neither achievable nor even desirable.

Evegeny Morozov,[37] a Harvard-educated Belarussian technology writer had this rather harsh description of enthusiasts:

The Web3 advocates remind me of those annoying vulgar Marxists who, for all the evidence to the contrary, kept insisting that the objective developments within capitalism favor the inevitable transition to socialism – only then to spend decades elaborating sophisticated templates, with plenty of vivid, utopian detail of what that inevitable arrival of socialism would be like. As a result, we have plenty of fascinating templates, but, somehow, the objective conditions for that transition are no longer there (if they ever were).

And so one of my eyebrows goes up here.

Consider today's Internet itself, as opposed to the Web (which uses it as a communication ecosystem). Owned by no one, the people's network, right? Uh-uh. Not even close to true. The network is a series of wireless connections, fibre connections, satellite connections, copper connections and servers sprinkled around the world acting as relay/routing stations to make sure that packets of bits get where they are supposed to go. Those connections, cables, fibre – they are all owned by either state or private corporations or non-profits, depending on the country. Similarly, the places where servers sit are governmental data centres or private data centres. There are hundreds of ways to choke off or censor the Internet, as we have seen in those countries who simply shut down traffic while bad stuff is happening internally or perhaps more darkly, only let in the stuff that they want their citizens to see, like China.

We have to accept that no amount of sovereign individual enthusiasm is going to build an end-to-end world owned by users and governed by tokens – at least in a world where they are competing with states and private enterprise.

To put this another way, and with my other eyebrow up: as long as there is capitalism and nation states, the utopian version of Web3 will be at least partially stunted.

* * *

There is a definitional confusion here which we must untangle. There is the Internet layer, which is the network that whips packages of bits from place to place. There is the Web layer, which allows easy access to the Internet and gives us things like browsers through which we access and interact with services (both of which are governed and advanced by various standards committees). And then there are the services themselves, sometimes called apps. (Go with me here: I know some apps don't use the Web at all, they skip that part and just use the underlying Internet directly.)

And I have just expressed some scepticism that the Internet layer and the Web layer will be able to become 'user-owned' and token-controlled anytime soon, although there are certainly people trying. It would require that the whole network and service layers manage to avoid the pressures of state and private enterprise and be redesigned to have a public blockchain architecture sitting at its base. That seems like a stretch.

But what of the applications themselves, the ones accessible from the Web or the App Store or Play Store? The Ubers and the Twitters and the Facebooks and the Amazons? There are already thousands of Web3 applications, although not of the scale of the big elephants. They use the Internet as their network, and use the Web as their user entry points, but then dart off to blockchains to do their stuff, with user private keys stored safely encrypted in a diplomatic crypto-pouch of sorts as they enter the smart contracts sitting on the blockchain. These Web3 apps are pretty much siloed at this point, they don't interact much with each other, and that is because a cryptotoken that gives certain rights on one Web 3 app does not always give it rights on another. Crypto currencies may flow seamlessly from Web3 app to Web3 app (because the widely used ones like Ether are a sort of lingua franca), but non-fungible tokens are by definition less portable; just like a ticket to a baseball game is not going to get you into the opera.

But this is all changing steadily and determinedly. The whole regime of crypto title ownership is sure to create strange bedfellows across entirely different offerings, it awaits the breeding of imaginative experiments, some of which will survive and thrive.

It feels like a recap is in order. I have somewhat incautiously divided the Internet into three layers (there are actually more, but again, simplicity reigns). There is the network layer and the web layer and the application layer. I have predicted that the rewiring of the network layer and/or web layer so that it embeds a centralized public blockchain with all its crypto magic is unlikely to happen, because it would facilitate the building of a ground-up ecosystem that can exclude state and business interests from the digital home where they have lived for over twenty years.

But the application layer – all those apps and services that we use daily – all are ripe for challenges to the old guard via a Web3 remake, because they can each break out and use blockchains and associated magic to facilitate cryptocurrency transactions and property rights. Which is great, except that 'portability' of these capabilities from Web3 app to Web3 app is still immature.

It is a hill to be climbed, but perhaps less steep than it seems.

Perhaps that's why, in the middle of 2022, Jack Dorsey of Twitter fame announced Web5. Why 5? Because his vision is Web3 + Web2. Some centralization, some decentralization.

A balance.

Chapter 16

THE NETWORK STATE

'A network state is a social network with a moral innovation, a sense of national consciousness, a recognized founder, a capacity for collective action, an in-person level of civility, an integrated cryptocurrency, a consensual government limited by a social smart contract, an archipelago of crowdfunded physical territories, a virtual capital, and an on-chain census that proves a large enough population, income, and real-estate footprint to attain a measure of diplomatic recognition.'

Balaji Srinivasan

We have already covered all of the major cross-currents of blockchain applications – NFTs, cryptocurrencies, DAOs, Metaverse, Gamefi and Web3. And while there is considerable overlap and intermingling (both NFTs and cryptocurrencies appear everywhere), they all represent different families of applications, and they have travelled some way along the maturity curve – real traction, real projects, real users, real ownership propositions.

We want to look at a project that doesn't exist, except as a hypothetical, a thought experiment, already being debated furiously amongst crypto-philosophers and political scientists.

It is called the Network State.

Balaji Srinivasan is an entrepreneur and one of this field's big thinkers. He was CTO of Coinbase and general partner at Andreessen Horowitz, both positions being of highest burnish for anyone. Balaji has been vocal on numerous matters around technology and society for a long time – when he talks, everyone listens. On 22nd July 2022 he published the eagerly anticipated book *The Network State*.[38] Its influence has rippled out well beyond technology and into philosophy, politics and economics.

The book spreads wide, but its proposition is simple, startling and, for most, a little over the top.

It builds on an article written in August 2011 by Marc Andreessen, co-founder of VC Andreessen Horowitz. It was in the *Wall Street Journal*, titled 'Software is Eating the World'. His central proposition was that *all* companies will be fuelled by software in the future, even those who are seemingly remote from nimble logic of bits. It may be obvious now, but it was not obvious to everyone back then.

Balaji's book goes way further, saying, 'software isn't done eating the world'. His narrative is simple. Software has allowed us to build our own companies like Airbnb, our own communities like Facebook, our own currencies like Bitcoin.

Now it is going to let us build our own countries.

Reading this assertion sparks a shower of objections. You mean as an equal to the US? France? South Korea? Competing and collaborating and engendering culture and loyalty and security and wealth creation and citizen fulfilment?

Yes, that is his central thesis.

And so he starts to build his case. In nation-states, he argues, the geography is primary and the ideology is secondary. I had always understood this differently, having believed that the nation-state was the caretaker of a cultural and political ideology. But as he convincingly points out,

Russia swapped out communism for nationalism without so much as a by-your-leave, while the geography stayed constant. Plenty of other examples come via war, revolution and the ballot box.

He compares the network state to an Ethereum conference, attended by many tens of thousands, where geography is irrelevant, attendees are remote, connected only by a shared belief. They gather, interact, have fun, make friends, share. All without common geography.

Consider that it is fairly common to find 'shared belief' groupings of many tens of millions or more on online via social media, often catalysed or founded by a small group of people, or even one person. Imagine then that twenty million people of like mind on some core issues of citizenry and culture, assembled as a collective. Imagine the bargaining power of such a group, especially if the group has economic power, plus its own cryptocurrency.

If you ignore geography, what you have is a virtual country. So why not negotiate for recognition as such? Passports and travel and the like? Objections well up again – the United Nations, armies that exist as a mechanism of violence against threats, taxes, etc. Balaji, in constructing this paradigm, addresses all of these.

Pause here to reread the opening part of the quote that leads this chapter again: 'A network state is a social network with a moral innovation, a sense of national consciousness, a recognized founder, a capacity for collective action, an in-person level of civility, an integrated cryptocurrency, a consensual government limited by a social smart contract...'

There are, of course, a series of layered arguments that brings him to a place in which he not only believes in the practicability of such a proposition, but more pointedly, to its inevitability.

For instance, Balaji references the Sovereign Individual, to whom we have devoted an entire chapter. It is not a huge jump of logic to now imagine a unified grouping of such individuals coalescing around a shared worldview. A Sovereign Collective, he calls it. And if one can imagine a Sovereign Collective, then the logical leap to 'country' status is simply a matter of numbers and bargaining power. Although I am mindful of the fact that the greater the number, the harder it might be to keep a monolithic worldview intact.

The two examples offered to prove his point about non-geographic collectives of shared worldviews are the pre-Israel Jewish diaspora, and the supporters of Islamic State, both externally cohesive cultural groupings without the benefit of borders.

Balaji is astoundingly well read, one of those polymaths that can extract fuel from any number of disciplines over millennia of history. I particularly like one purposefully mixed metaphor in support of his arguments. He dredges up Leviathan, a many-headed monster originating from the Old Testament in the Book of Isaiah, but put into service of Greek mythology; a huge scary sea monster whose bidding you would be well advised to follow. Balaji presents us with three Leviathans driving prosocial behaviour throughout the arc of history.

The first was a transcendent God. People behaved in a prosocial manner mainly out of a fear of displeasing God and getting whumped upside the head in the afterlife. Or even before the afterlife. As religion and superstition started to lose their grip, the nation-state stepped in as the next Leviathan (think of the English Papists being forced out by the King of England as a good example). You also do not want to mess with these people, the officers of the state. They will put you in prison and worse for antisocial behaviour. We do not steal partially for that reason, mixed in, I suppose with some good old hand-me-down religious morality. But, of course, in nation-states people do steal and sometimes get away with it, and the state does sometimes seize stuff.

But his third and newest Leviathan is a far more gentle creature. It is advanced technology. It is maths. It is cryptographically protected property rights. It is what we have talked about for sixteen chapters. You don't steal because you can't. The maths won't allow it. You don't need God or the nation state to threaten you. Antisocial behaviour runs into the wall of cryptography and smart contracts.

You need a great deal of philosophical rope to let this pass without contestation, obviously. But I like the argument. It is indeed true that cryptographically secured property rights acts as a bulwark to theft and seizure. Not everything, obviously – I can still theoretically use physical violence to take what is not mine. But crypto gives certainty to provenance, and that is the point. Ownership is secured, even if the owned object is snatched. Once provenance is completely locked by mathematics, theft and seizure become much harder.

It is obviously a broad debate, with no small amount of snarky derision and breathless admiration pouring from all corners, particularly after Balaiji's book and subsequent blogs and YouTube and podcasts appearances. Balaji was basically swatting away the entire history of human societal and communal evolution and saying – *I have a better idea because of some fine new maths.* But nation-states are very powerful, especially the ones with both democracies and bombs. One needs to try hard to imagine an alternative that would not be met with concerted resistance, and smothered at birth. On the other hand, the very first stirrings are being seen and heard.

There is CityDAO, for instance, in which forty physical acres were purchased in rural Wyoming (of course) and people were invited to apply for passports which were issued via NFTs. That gives city residents a right to vote on how land is to be used and governed, as well as being given the right to purchase land at some future date when more can be acquired. Not a whole lot of pizzazz here, given that the land is in a real country, and so has superseding laws. Also, CityDAO has not met its projections. They have 5,000 members, about half of their forecasts. Still, an interesting early experiment.

Then there is PraxisSociety, which was seed-funded by Balaji and had a second round of funding in March of 2022, which included some big names in venture capital. Their vision statement as you enter the website is aspirational:

Technology gives us the opportunity to build better cities, founded on community and shared values. In the 20th century, cities were organized around labor markets. Now, we can work remote from anywhere we choose. With this new freedom, we can leave work-centric cities and live with people who share our values. Praxis is leading this movement. We are building a new city, organized around vitality.

Praxis is a society of future city residents, ranging from founders, creatives, investors, and all in-between. Our membership is application-based. Once accepted, members attend events and can participate in the building of the city. Most importantly, members have a shared way of life: optimism, good health, clear purpose, and commitment to an idea greater than themselves, encapsulated in a word: Vitality.

Many new city projects begin with construction, then search for residents. Praxis inverts this process: we built the community first. Together, we're building the city where we want to live.

As much as I want to buy into this vision, there is a quasi-religious feel to it which makes me nervous. Reading the preceding paragraphs with a jaundiced eye immediately sees a shimmer of cults, or something near that. There is, of course, a tight coupling to our central proposition – that of a sovereign currency and secure property rights, but I struggle to see this as enough of a differentiator to avoid its proximity to some very dark events in recent history. What starts as a 'common moral worldview' can easily unravel into a become fundamentalist nightmare.

Still, there are some very important thinkers and financiers taking this very seriously. The most important of these, at least with respect to his influence, is Vitalek Buterin, who wrote a long blog[39] soon after Balaji's missive. He was generally supportive but gently pushed back on some of the details.

Vitalek quickly signalled a thumbs-up, observing that network states 'can be viewed as attempts to sketch out a bigger political narrative for crypto'. Vitalek is deeply concerned with 'public goods'; it is a thread through much of his writing. He has clearly grown impatient with the culture of fast money and asset prices (although not completely, I presume), and seems to be far more excited by the political and philosophical implications of blockchain and its potential to do good for the world. But unlike Balaji, who is an extreme zero-regulation libertarian, Vitalek is somewhat more centrist, getting dangerously close to being an old-style liberal.

He proposed what he calls the Big Compromise, arguing that a pure libertarian view of life, such as those espoused by Balaji's Network State, run into the big problem of how to fund 'public goods', which are best handled by a benevolent centre. He proposed (as examples), such as Universal Basic Income, a land tax or a cap on too much wealth concentration, channelling a sort of Bernie Sanders view of politics for this new vision of a techno-secured and governed country. He even proposes (gasp!) a democratic vote rather than token-controlled governance.

There is a great comparison between his view and Balaji's near the end of Vitalek's blog:

> Generally, I am used to the Big Compromise Idea being a leftist one: some form of equality and democracy. Balaji, on the other hand, has Big Compromise Ideas that feel more rightist: local communities with shared values, loyalty, religion, physical environments structured to encourage personal discipline ('keto kosher') and hard work. These values are implemented in a very libertarian and tech-forward way, organizing not around land, history, ethnicity and country, but around the cloud and personal choice, but they are rightist values nonetheless. This style of thinking is foreign to me, but I find it fascinating, and important.

Balaji's response (I paraphrase)? *Thank you for taking this seriously. Yeah, this is just a working set of ideas for a manifesto. Edits welcome!*

Indeed. And as Vitalek points out, the promise is indeed fascinating. It takes us well beyond asset prices and NFTs and Metaverses and into the possibility that our mathematical curiosity – the trapdoor function – will paint civilization anew.

It is an easy matter to laugh at all of this.. But it is a tantalizing thought.

Chapter 17

OIL AND WATER –
STABLECOINS AND CBDCs

Here is where the gloves come off. CBDCs (Central Bank Digital Currencies) and Stablecoins are entirely different creatures, save for perhaps using some overlapping technological plumbing and their shared aspirations to be stable and frictionless instruments of digital currency. The reason why I am slamming together these polar opposites in the same chapter is to highlight the winds of war now starting to howl – the battle between personal ownership of money and state ownership of money. And as importantly, what happens to programmable money if it is abused.

Let's start with a quote:

> You could think of giving your children pocket money, but programming the money so that it couldn't be used for sweets. There is a whole range of things that money could do, programmable money, which we cannot do with the current technology.

It is a fairly simple journey from this tiny example of *programmable money* to the prospect of it being used for social control over a much wider and darker terrain. Bought too many beers at the liquor store? No public transport for you for a month. Ate too much at the restaurant? Sorry, you can only buy rice until further notice and are banned from restaurants for a month. Paid for a magazine we don't like? Sorry, we are closing your bank account.

If this seems a little too dystopian to be taken seriously, consider China. They have already implemented widespread social control and punishment through a nationwide network of cameras, digital snooping and its near-total control of electronic payment infrastructure. Financial punishment for small infractions like camera-captured jaywalking are now widespread. Punishment and social isolation for larger infractions, like even fairly benign anti-government posts, are similarly widespread, including total social isolation.

China has had these thumbscrews in place for some time, well before crypto caught fire; the consequence of advanced tech and AI and machine learning all press-ganged in the service of a hatchet-faced autocracy dedicated to keeping one billion citizens from personal freedom's corrupting influences.

And now China is rolling out the digital yuan (named the e-CNY). Twenty-three cities were brought into the fold in September 2022, with a timeline for the entire country now on track. It is not hard to see what will happen. Firstly, citizen payments are not anonymous. Anonymity is one of the hallmarks of cash. Someone with a note in their pocket can spend freely and privately, without having to explain motive to anyone. Not so with the e-CNY. Secondly, the e-CNY is programmable. And that program can be changed at any time, without citizen consultation. In other words, your e-CNY may be different from mine. It is not really fungible.

Cash differs there too – its usage is locked and committed to single purpose and is completely fungible.

There is almost no one who expects the Chinese to respect anonymity and privacy as the e-CNY starts to eclipse traditional payment instruments. Neither is there any expectation that CCP would not use programmability as a tool of social control, all the way down to individual citizen level. It is not only dystopian and terrifying, but a near-certainty in that authoritarian nation-state.

Yes, but that's China, you may argue, it could never happen in a state more respectful of citizen's rights. Before I push back on this view, take a look again at the quote at the beginning of the chapter.

That was spoken not in China or some other dictatorship, but by Sir Jon Cunliffe, deputy governor of the Bank of England.[40]

He added, 'There can be some socially beneficial outcomes, which prevent activity that is seen as socially harmful in one way or another. But at the same time, it could be a restriction on people's freedoms.'

He was suggesting that the government would need to look into the possibility of spend-control as a social matter, and make a determination. More concerningly, he expressed no preference for a particular outcome.

The hairs on my back went up when I read this in February 2022. Why did I react so strongly? I mean, this was England after all. The public would never put up with such intrusions, right? But the public already does. Nations, as we have previously mentioned, have central banks (often only nominally independent from government) who can and do make decisions to print money as a tool to achieve national economic goals, when necessary. This has been true in our very recent past, which has resulted in inflation, most notably in the US. And that (with certainty) debases the purchasing power of citizens' money. One need only ask an Argentinian or Turkish citizen how their money fared over the past ten years to see how close inflation is to a citizen's immediate concerns. Of course, sometimes the central bank goes the other way, sucking liquidity out of the economy, which creates a whole set of other outcomes. Or increasing and decreasing interest rates.

Those are the two levers of central banks (money supply and interest rates), which are juggled and twiddled to try and keep prices stable and employment high. And the reason they get to do this is because the government *owns* the money and delegates its control to the central bank. It is not the citizens who own their money, even if they think they do, at least during good times. But during bad times, the government makes their ownership and control deafeningly clear. The juggling and twiddling of a nation's finances does not always work as intended, as evidenced from thousands of years of history.

CBDCs will vastly increase the efficacy of central control of money supply and spend, and increase the velocity of capital through the economy. While there were a number of CBDC projects that did not use blockchain, most of those since 2020 have appropriated some of the ingredients of blockchain to secure their ecosystems, but without having to concern themselves with distractions like permissionlessness or public consensus or decentralization or privacy. It allows them to efficiently and quickly mint, distribute, clear and settle to whatever purpose they deem will produce the economic results they require. All without giving up the centralized control on which they feed. Of course banks don't necessarily have to use blockchains to do this, but of the over one hundred countries now planning or rolling out CBDCs, most will be using private blockchains, because the open-source ethos of blockchain has provided a wealth of pre-tested and hardened blocks of functional code and has made blockchain technology the obvious choice. The irony of which is not lost on me – the innovations of the progenitors of blockchain were looking to escape from centralized financial control, and have now inadvertently handed over a copy of the tools to allow the powers-that-be to defend their turf.

They haven't even said thank you.

So there are multiple layers of threat. There is the threat of social control, and there is also the threat of passive financial surveillance, which, even if not acted upon, will have a chilling effect on our understanding of privacy. And of course, the threat of a machine that allows instantaneous implementation of financial policy by unelected officials, even if that policy is flawed. This last threat is not new, but with blockchain magic, it is easier to do (remember the complexity and the energy expended on the US national stimulus checques during Covid?). Simple with digital currency, direct from central bank to citizens without commercial bank intermediaries. All of this is being put into play with essentially no consultation with the users of money – us. Other than the periodic offering of a ballot box, at least in democracies, which does not always make much of a difference to the central bank and its governors.

* * *

The history of stable digital currency within the banking fraternity goes back to well before Bitcoin, with the first real implementation having been the Avant in Finland in early 1990s, followed by I LIKE Q in Czechia in 2000, but as innovative and as short-lived as these programs were, they were simply digital copies of existing currencies, and interchangeable with them. None of the benefits of today's blockchain were part of these experiments, particularly with respect to consensus and digital signatures and carefully considered armoury against double-spend and other malfeasance.

In fact, it was only with the inflow of retail capital into the Bitcoin and Ethereum ecosystems that both central and commercial banks heard a whisper of threat. One could just imagine a 2017 meeting at the Bank of International Settlements (a pan-global organization which acts as the banker and co-ordinator for central bank collaboration), in which a probably mild-mannered Swiss banker raised the issue to a sceptical room full of suits. This thing is accruing value, he would have said. And being used as a store of that value, and even for payment. And hundreds of billions have flowed into it in a few years, he might have informed them. Quickly. And accelerating. We need to respond, because if this continues...

Who knows. It was not recorded. But what happened very quickly was that everyone from the BIS to commercial banks to regulators quickly sat up and started to take notice. Position papers were written. BIS in 2020. WEF in 2021. National banks, regional banks, local banks, lawmakers, regulators, policy institutes, oversight committees, watchdog organizations, industry bodies, law firms. Everyone seemed to wake up on the same morning saying – Good God, what are we going to do about this?

And what they decided was stark. There is a threat to us. It is crypto. We must take what we can from the open-source pool of treasures, and build our own and legislate aggressively against the rest, because we do not want to give up on the ritual of state-owned money and compliant citizenry. Even if we lose. Slow it down, obfuscate facts. Blame someone. Scare the public. We have too much to lose.

If I sound a little tetchy, it is because I am. So let me slow down, take a breath and turn to stablecoins – which absolutely do cleave to our blinking star of immutable individual ownership of money.

Stablecoins have a bullseye on their backs. Everyone from Christine Lagarde from the European Central Bank to legacy investor Warren Buffet has been scathing, even shrill. Insults have been, er, colourful. Buffet called all of crypto 'rat poison squared'. Lagarde, using more measured language said, 'Using stablecoins as a store of value could trigger a large shift of bank deposits to stablecoins, which may have an impact on banks' operations and the transmission of monetary policy.'

Of course. That's rather the point. If it is indeed true that I can access a value-stable currency and securely own it, and use it to buy all the stuff that I usually buy, and am able to send it to who I please, and never have to deal with a bank again or pay transaction fees or wait for settlement while you steal my float, then hell yeah, it will certainly have an impact on banks' operations.

If you were sitting on the other side of that last paragraph you would be reactive too. You would say – an unmonitored private currency creates systemic risk. I would respond, an unconstrained state currency has shown itself to have unacceptable risk too. Ask a Turk or Argentinian, or even a UK or US citizen circa October 2022.

* * *

Let's back up. The first stablecoin pegged to the value of the dollar was the DAI, created by Rune Christensen in a project launched by him called Maker and pegged exactly to the value of one dollar (more on this mechanism later). This was in 2017. Why did he want a stablecoin? There were two reasons, somewhat interlinked. The first was related to the price volatility of other assets in crypto – Ethereum, Bitcoin, etc. In a world of chaotic swings of price, it seemed prudent to create a cryptocurrency that had no swings in price. Again, why? Because it would allow crypto players to enter and exit other crypto assets *without withdrawing funds to and from an old-style bank*. Again, why? Because of banking fees and time. If value was safely sitting in a dollar-pegged crypto currency parked in the cryptosphere, one could use the stablecoin to zip around the cryptosphere, swapping it for other currencies, NFTs, whatever. Instantaneously and cheaply, which are not words one ever applies to a bank.

So speed and cost of deployment and price protection was a catalyst. But there was another related reason. Any value held in stablecoin was a *predictable* asset because of its calm temperament, price-wise. It could be used for all sorts of purposes that require long term prudence, like collateral against loans. And Maker was also the first true lend/borrow project in Defi, so there was incentive for Christensen to launch a stablecoin.

Since this launch, there has been an explosion of stablecoins based on varying underlying principles – 97 at the time of writing. Although only ten have market caps of over $500 million, and only five have market caps of $1 billion or more, with a stablecoin called Tether (reasonably old as established) having top spot at over $80 billion at the time of writing.

At the risk of repeating myself, stablecoins are critical to the crypto ecosystem because they are reasonably price-predictable, they have a common language ('pegged' to the price of a dollar, or some other well-known asset), they are very liquid and frictionless to move around the crypto eco-system, and can be easily transported to-and-from the fiat world. Liquidity is the nuclear fuel of all finance. If assets are illiquid (in crypto or in the real world), it is like being stuck in mud. By the time you have unstuck yourself, prices may have moved against you. Just think about the value of a house that you may own. To turn that into dollars for some other purpose is a *very* long process. Stablecoins are much easier rails on which all assets in the crypto universe can glide.

And what is the most important thing about stablecoins? They can be securely owned. It is the immutable, non-seizable property of the owner. Unlike a dollar, which is vulnerable to the arbitrary policies of a government. As we have said earlier, they can be seized, debased and debauched without much recourse for the holder.

The details of how the stablecoins maintain their parity with the price of the dollar are interesting and quite technical (and for some stablecoins, deep in mathematical weeds). Suffice it to say that some stablecoins have essentially one dollar (or equivalent) in the bank for every stablecoin sold, and others use fancy algorithms and arbitrage and other enticements to the crypto markets to keep them stable. And amongst this second set, there have been some utterly sensational failures, including a $40 billion meltdown of a stablecoin called Terra in May 2021, which had the unfortunate effect of acting as a red flag to the regulator bulls and a loud and gleeful I-told-you-so from the crypto-sceptical world.

These events have been widely covered in the media, as has the difference between the so-called collateralized stablecoins and the algorithmic stablecoins. It is a noisy space, which obfuscates a much more important narrative that we should analyse.

Let us assume for a moment that there is only one stablecoin, fully collateralized by dollars held in a bank somewhere, usable as currency across the entire crypto space and redeemable for those real dollars at the behest of the owner. Let us further assume that the size of the entire crypto market is $1.5 trillion (it has been as high as $3 trillion in late 2021). Let us also assume that the issuer of this stablecoin pays an interest rate 1% point higher than real world banks (because the cost base of a smart contract allows them to compete favourably with human-heavy banks with profit incentives).

This raises the obvious question. Why would you ever leave your money in a bank again? The stablecoin is owned by you, the money in the bank is owned by the state. The stablecoin is getting you a somewhat higher interest rate than a bank. You can swap for dollars if you need to, at parity. And if the bank goes bankrupt, you still have your stablecoins. You do not have to fill out forms. There is no minimum. And if the state starts to print dollars, making you nervous of inflation, just swap for a Euro or Singaporean dollar stablecoin, instantaneously, without asking permission, at almost negligible cost. And of course, the stablecoin is available to trade anything within the cryptosphere.

Under such conditions, there would be *no* reason to hold dollars in a traditional bank. The only reason that everyone is not already doing this is that the crypto industry is still new and distrusted and misunderstood and difficult to navigate, and critically, underregulated.

But central banks and commercial banks and regulators, at least the savviest of them, know that the value proposition of *trusted* stablecoin will be much more attractive to a citizen than a dollar. $1.5 trillion is big enough to threaten the traditional banking market, if that amount (and more in the future) were to disappear permanently from the traditional banking system. And so we have regulatory tanks and rocket launchers being rolled out.

That state and its commercial banking partners cannot abide the citizen owning their own money, it is a direct loss of control. So they are going to compete. They are going to roll out CBDCs. Fast, liquid, secure, immutable and all that other fine stuff. Plus they will tell you that it is backed by the 'full faith and credit' of the state, for whatever that is worth (more meaningless words I cannot imagine in a world of unpredictable global capital).

But you still won't own it. And this is where the battle will be fought.

Chapter 18

HEADWINDS

The journey for mass adoption of blockchain-borne applications has been mainly uphill, at least so far. This has not been true of most of the other transformative technologies over the last century. Take any – TV, computers, transistors, the PC, mobile phones, the Internet. Even those that have strayed onto contentious territory like CRISPR and AI (whose detractors have raised ethical concerns for at least some of their applications), have been widely welcomed by scientists, technologists and public alike.

Not crypto.

I have been puzzled by this for a while. Pushback has come from everywhere. Not only in the centres of power mentioned in this book, like financial and governmental, but also from the media and from the public at large. Just about the only place crypto has found welcoming passage is in academia, where one assumes that the magic of the cryptography and other algorithms that secure and operate the blockchain receive the admiration they deserve.

But on closer inspection perhaps it is not that puzzling.

Some of the other transformative technologies I have mentioned received little pushback, but were often largely ignored until they weren't. Remember when the Internet first appeared in our peripheral vision? Not many people took notice of that either, including Microsoft which ignored it until 1995 when Bill Gates wrote his famous 'tidal wave' internal memo[41], completely turning his huge ship around to sail on the waves of the Internet and his Explorer browser, calling it the 'the most important single development to come along since the PC'.

And the first smartphone, BlackBerry. I remember people saying, why would I want to get my emails on a tiny screen with a tiny keyboard? And then Apple came along and built a whole ecosystem and people finally got it.

But blockchain's position in this pantheon of technology's great societal transformers still seems to have few believers. Perhaps this is why: the PC was easy to explain, even though most people thought it was a hobby for nerds at first. The Internet was easy to explain, although most people thought that they would have little use for it. The smartphone was easy to explain, although most people did not foresee it becoming so central to our lives that we now spend hours per day doing one of many things presented on its screen.

But the blockchain is simply not that easy to explain. Neither is cryptography and what it does, why it is important and how it will affect our daily lives (other than some vague waffle about 'security'). Worse, the industry has been painted in the lurid colours of fortunes made and lost, of huge wads of money stolen in seconds, of energy used and regulators roiled. And then there were the additional ingredients of the fast money that was made by early adoptees, many of them simply lucky, and the somewhat annoying 'maxis' who tout their favourite blockchain projects as though it was a team sport.

Most of the narrative around crypto has been tainted with the fact that the very first application, Bitcoin, was about money, and only about money (or payment, to be more specific). And so it brought out the basest of reactions, as money often does. Had the very first application been a token which provided a democratic governance vote in a DAO or a secure NFT-based DNS address, I suspect that there would have been no pushback at all. They would have been considered interesting curiosities, at least at first.

The other big technologies over the last fifty years were not about money (although a great deal of wealth was created by their subsequent commercialization). The first blockchain was not only all about money, but it also wasn't clear to most people in *which way* it was about money. And then when non-financial crypto-assets started appearing, it became even more confusing – if these are not cryptocurrencies, then what are they? Throw all of this obfuscation, misinterpretation, proximity to wealth, wild hucksterism, unregulated jungles and threats to power centres, and what do you get?

Detractors and non-believers and haters and resistors.

Which brings us to this author's problem. I am spending hundreds of pages trying to articulate this magical new form of ownership, a revolution at the core of how societies function. But it's simply not as sexy as Jennifer Doudna's CRISPR or Job's first iPhone or Tim Berners-Lee's World Wide Web. I don't really even have an identified person to tie it to.

Nevertheless...

Let's get more granular about the headwinds, most of which I predict will eventually subside.

* * *

We have talked fairly extensively about the regulatory pushback and some moves being made by various governments.

On the positive side of the spectrum, as discussed earlier we have seen the Law Commission in the UK 'get it', but it is just a consultation paper, with no guarantee that it will end up in law. In other jurisdictions we have seen various clumsy attempts to shoehorn crypto into creaking early twentieth century regulation. And there have been, as widely reported, outright bans and threats.

Regulation is a broad canvas, particularly when it comes to matters of money and value (as opposed to health or environment, for instance). So here are the main areas where regulators efforts are focused:

- Asset Classification – is the thing a security, a currency, financial asset, a commodity, a property, a collectible? All of these have different sets of regulations (and are different in different geographies).
- Asset Geography – where is the asset, for regulation purposes? If someone has Bitcoin the blockchain, where is it? Where did the funds come from to purchase it? What happens when it returns to fiat in a different geography?
- Tax – asset classification determines tax treatment. Tax profits on crypto disposal when returning to fiat? Should tax be imposed within cryptosphere-only transactions? Are tax losses in crypto a thing? What if I simply leave it in a wallet and give my daughter the private key? What about donations or barter (I give you my Steinway piano, you give me Bored Ape, no reporting necessary)?
- Anti-Money Laundering – how does the state ensure that the source of funds is not illicit? How does it identify the owner of crypto when the entire point of some crypto projects is anonymity? While states can (and do) force

exchanges to impose AML processes, once the funds are in the cryptoverse, they can move around anonymously. Can they and should they be followed?

- Advertising – when is it permitted, when is it legit, when is it misleading?
- Stablecoins – how does the state control this, especially when users can buy airline tickets and property directly with stablecoins? How does the state see capital flowing through the economy if it is not bank issued and spent in legal entities?
- Liability – who is in the firing line for blame when things go bad – project leaders? Token-holders? DAOs? Software developers?

There are certainly other regulatory threads, but the problem should be obvious. It is hard enough to harmonize and monitor and implement these sorts of regulations in the physical world (think of tech companies setting up in low-tax geographies to escape local tax encumbrances), but to work out how to do this in a space where often anonymous assets were imagined into existence a mere twelve years ago seems like an impossible task.

And yet there are a lot of smart people trying. The Work Economic Forum (WEF) produced a call to action June 2022, broad and urgent, titled 'The Macroeconomic Impact of Cryptocurrency and Stablecoins'[42]. But they are also an influencer in upcoming EU Parliament legislation. They report:

At the end of June 2022, the Council presidency and the European Parliament reached a provisional agreement on the markets in crypto assets (MiCA) proposal which covers issuers of unbacked crypto assets, and stablecoins, as well as the trading venues and wallets where crypto assets are held. This regulatory framework is intended to protect investors and preserve financial stability while allowing innovation and fostering the attractiveness of the crypto asset sector. The purpose of MiCA is to provide more clarity across the European Union, as some member states already have varying national legislation for crypto assets, but there had been no specific regulatory framework at an EU level.

In October the full legal language was approved, and was promulgated in April 2023. And following immediately on the heels of this is the proposed Digital Commodities Consumer Protection Act (DCCPA) in the US, which is similarly well researched and seeking to punch its way through the horse-trading and special interests of US lawmaking. Add to this the March 2023 'Economic Report of the President', an annual publication by the US Council of Economic which included an entire chapter on digital assets and 'economic principles', an ominous warning shot across the bows – we are taking this very seriously.

The language in these documents is a tad stiff, and the details pretty stultifying, but the message is clear. Regulation needs to happen and happen quickly. Of course, the WEF and their influential friends are closely connected to exactly those centres of power that have the most to lose from crypto. So speed is not a bad idea.

But that, of course, is an aspiration, and until then, there is an alternative approach, mainly being employed in the US. It is more brutalist and it is this – charge people under old laws, intimidate them with threats of fines and prisons and let the courts decide, and lob the ball back into the legislators' court.

The latter half of 2022 brought an accelerating series of these enforcement actions against companies and individuals by the SEC and CFTC (Securities Exchange Commission and the Commodities Futures Trading Commission) in the US. I choose the US to make a larger point, but this theatre is playing out worldwide. The action is aimed at project founders, corporations, LLCs, DAOs and even Kim Kardashian, who paid a fine for shilling a rubbish cryptocurrency called EthereumMax that came and went without a trace.

And so we have to mention two regulators, Hester Pierce and Summer Mersinger. Pierce is an SEC commissioner. Her boss is Gary Gensler, head of the SEC, and famously threatening of the crypto industry. He is leading a charge of enforcement actions against those projects which he has determined have sold tokens without having registered them as securities first. The actions of his agency have been confusing even to his own commissioners. He has said Bitcoin is not a security. He has said that Ether is not a security, later backtracking into mixed signals. He has said that other tokens are 'probably' securities, even though some of them operate on the same principles as Bitcoin or Ethereum. Nobody seems to have real clarity on his views or policies. One might argue that whatever laws do exist are a mess, and so his approach to market regulation is simply a reflection of that.

Pierce seems to agree that her agency is getting it wrong. She has gotten a little pissed off in the past. In the most diplomatic of terms, of course. But she said in at least one interview with Coindesk: 'The SEC is a regulatory agency with an enforcement division, not an enforcement agency. Why are we leading with enforcement actions in crypto?'

Ouch. She couldn't have been much clearer. The regulatory approach of the SEC seems chaotic and knee-jerky, and it is damaging an industry which has enormous potential. It is a gale of a headwind.

It doesn't stop there though. There has been somewhat of a turf war in the US about who should regulate crypto, and that war is ongoing. It remains a little opaque. SEC is going to regulate security matters and CFTC is going to regulate commodity matters, and because no one has decided what a crypto asset is and isn't, crypto is under regulatory surveillance and threat all over the place with both agencies taking increasingly aggressive action on enforcement.

Just like the SEC, the CFTC have a gadfly in their midst. She is Summer Mersinger. She said of her agency's recent action against a DAO, in what has accurately been defined as a 'stinging dissent', that the agency should have engaged in formal rulemaking on DAO liability rather than engaging in blatant 'regulation by enforcement'.

These two examples are just more of the same ground we have trodden previously in this book, but what is different here is the very confusedness and uncertainty itself whips up the headwind. No one knows what to do. Investors stay away. Projects and their creators look nervously over their shoulders. Funding becomes fraught. Even token holders feel targeted. In many ways, I would argue, incomplete or uncertain regulation is worse than bad regulation. Regulation moves at the speed of government, which even in the most efficient of countries is bogged down by maddening processes. Tech innovation is on the opposite spectrum. It simply withers when slowed down. Some lawmakers know this, and are pushing hard to keep the flame alive, but the vast majority of those in control of the legislative pens are blocked by their own misunderstanding of the technology and its promise.

Which brings us to the next headwind – this stuff is complex to understand.

* * *

Let's say it again. Blockchains and the whole crypto enterprise is befuddling. Let me give an example from my own immersion in the field. There is a branch of crypto maths called zero-knowledge proofs. I would guess that the number of people in the entire world who knew about zero-knowledge proofs from the ground up before crypto arrived was in the many hundreds or so. Now there are probably tens of thousands.

Why? Because zero-knowledge proofs not only will make some blockchains 1000 times faster (or more), but they will also start to get applied to stuff other than blockchains. If you ask me how they work, I will give you a stumbling and likely inaccurate answer, because zero-knowledge proofs seem like an impossible magic trick. So here goes – it is a mathematical structure that proves that a statement is true or false without ever having to reveal to external parties how it did it. It's 100% trustworthy. An example? You say to the taxman – this is what I owe you, you really don't have to ever see my financial records, you can trust me and my zero-knowledge maths (and they can, that's the magic!).

As interesting as this sidebar may be, the larger point is that this entire field is dripping with jargon that almost no one understands. Public key infrastructure, tokenomics, consensus algorithms, hard forks, soft forks, hard wallets, soft wallets, multisig, digital signatures, Merkle trees, Layer 0,

Layer 1, Layer 2, Layer 3, trilemma dilemma, zero-knowledge rollups, optimistic rollups, ERC-20, gas, airdrops. The entire glossary of inscrutable terms in the crypto world would fill a number of tomes.

And the rest of us don't really care. We simply want a good return on our savings or a cheap loan or reliable insurance or simply comfort that no one is going to forge our car registration or title deed to our house. Or someone we can call and speak to when something untoward happens. Like the customer support line, even if it is occasionally painful.

This is perhaps where the greatest headwinds howl. While techno-literates may rejoice in their mastery of this stuff, most people simply do not have the telemetry and bandwidth to spare. Even those of us who have learned to use the now familiar web for things which previously required physical interaction are sometimes on the losing side of this. I once booked a complex multi-moving part vacation abroad with my family – all online, a considerable saving, no travel agent commissions. I was very proud of myself. I did the whole thing without talking to a single human. Cars, trains, hotels, flights, sightseeing tours, hikes. And then, when we had arrived in the foreign country it was hit with the worst unreasonable snowstorm in their history. There was no one to call. We camped in a tiny hotel room for a week, eating bland sandwiches (sent up from an ever-shrinking kitchen supply) and watching TV in a foreign language. We had no way of leaving, all roads and rail and air traffic was closed. A travel agent would have found a way. And we lost all of our deposits, everywhere.

So now to David Birch[43]. He is somewhat of a celebrity in a rarefied space. He is UK-based author, speaker, consultant, podcaster, specializing in the subject of digital money and identity. There are plenty of those in the crypto space, but David has been doing this for far longer than crypto's young life. His books have received rave reviews, been foreworded by luminaries like Andrew Haldane, Chief Economist at the Bank of England, and praised by uber-economists like Kenneth Rogoff. The people who trust him, take his advice and put him on their boards are largely the big institutions that we have spent some time lightly lambasting in this book.

I can see why. I spoke to him via Zoom sometime in late 2022 – he is smart, funny and convincing in a way that only someone who has seen it all can be. Given that he swims in a pool with both old-guard corporate types (including many bankers) and opinionated young crypto enthusiasts, his equanimity is likely the lifebuoy that keeps him afloat.

Unsurprisingly, he is sceptical of much, although not all, in the crypto space.

Take cryptocurrencies. He made a point which brought me up short. On the subject of crypto's non-inflationary autonomous monetary systems (which is famously assumed to be a plus), he asked me to imagine that Bitcoin was the only global currency. Who is going to turn on the printers when there is a national need for emergency liquidity, like a pandemic or a global climate catastrophe? he asked. I didn't have a good answer for that.

What does he like about the blockchain? He particularly admires the startling clearing and settlement efficiencies and concomitant improvement in costs and speed. He is similarly enthusiastic about tokens as an efficient mechanism of trade. Tokens can move between stakeholders effortlessly, trading securely and quickly and without any of the friction of legacy processes. The ability to tether tokens to stocks or derivatives or real estate or anything else is something that he sees as, well, rather impressive. David is measured, not given to hyperbole, and he might not actually have said 'rather impressive', but that seems to fit. Oh, and he likes the financial transparency on offer in Defi. I nodded enthusiastically when he said that.

What about the headwinds we have discussed so far? This is where David revs up a bit. People are never going to be their own bank, he says, slapping away the fondest hopes of some Defi praise singers. There is a reason for banks and exchanges and the like. They didn't drop from the sky, he says. They offer a service, there are the layers of expertise and customer support that protect us from having to learn stuff we have no interest in learning (here he regales me with a funny anecdote about his pension advisor trying to explain to him the arcana of pension funds, laws, tax, annuities and other 'twiddle' in which he had no interest).

I had always assumed that these particular headwinds – ease of use, user experience, simplicity of message – would be overcome by the arts of UI and comms. Designing a financial journey would be as easy as ordering an Uber or booking an Airbnb. I am not so sure after speaking to David.

And on our central narrative? The ownership proposition enabled by the blockchain. David got that. He liked it.

I thus emerged relatively unscathed from our chat.

* * *

I had intended to be silent on the topic of energy usage, given that I believe it to be an issue that (sticking to our headwinds metaphor) is simply overblown. But given its prominence in crypto misinformation, I will be brief.

It is not a question of how much energy is used in the mining process (Bitcoin dominates here with its energy-intensive mining approach). It is a question of whether the energy used is concomitant with its value to humanity. Bitcoin mining uses the same order of magnitude of energy as the cruise industry. The cruise industry services about 150,000 reasonably affluent customers and cannot scale. Bitcoin serves over 100 million people and is scaling rapidly. And provides the most hardened global payment rails in history. No one has a problem with the cruise industry, which clearly is less important to humanity than a globally inclusive, uncensorable and secure payment ecosystem.

60% of the energy now used for mining is produced from green sources. The Mac Air I am typing on, my iPhone and my car and my fridge are below 40% green. Bitcoin mining is the cleanest industrial usage of energy in the world.

The majority of Bitcoin mining occurs in areas of over-abundant energy supply (like hydro); it is not using energy that could be used elsewhere. The potential energy would otherwise simply go unused.

A recent paper by Michel Khazzaka titled 'Bitcoin: Cryptopayments Energy Efficiency'[44] is the first extensive apples-apples comparison between financial transactions in the physical world (cash, credit cards, Internet banking, etc). It concluded that Bitcoin payments are fifty-six times more energy efficient than equivalent fiat transactions. The research is deep and extensive and convincing and goes even further. If the Lightning Network is used (a set of payment rails sitting on top of Bitcoin), the energy efficiency is 1,000,000 times that of an equivalent fiat transaction.

At the risk of tempting blowback, the people who are most

vocal about the energy usage in Bitcoin mining are people who simply don't like Bitcoin (many of the breathless reports on energy usage were funded by financial institutions). This is not an argument worth having, because facts cease to matter, and ideology takes over.

This headwind will surely subside, but in the interim those who invest in Bitcoin mining operations are taking heed, aware that politics plays as much of a role in investing as does technology and profits. The race to green mining is a matter of competitive urgency for these companies, most of whom have signed on to the Crypto Climate Accord of 2020, which commits to a net-zero carbon footprint by 2030, and who seek ever more energy efficient solutions, which directly aligns with the profit incentive (the lower the energy cost, the higher the profit of the miner).

Chapter 19

GRIFT

The discussion around bad actors in the crypto ecosystem was going to be the last section of the previous chapter, joining the already considerable headwinds of regulation and complexity.

But literally within seconds of sitting down to write, my iPhone pinged and I glanced down and read of a $560 million hack of a cryptocurrency called BinanceCoin (BNB), which is one of the top five cryptocurrencies by market cap. The details of this hack will no doubt be excavated with rigour over the next few weeks. They may get the funds back, they may get some of the funds back, they may get none. The perp or perps may be caught, they may not, and if they don't they may not be able to launder the stolen loot. There is even a growing class of near-riskless crimes in which the hacker contacts the project from whom they just stole and says, I will give back 90% of the coins and tell you how I did. I keep the 10% for revealing the vulnerability, you should thank me and indemnify me. And this is repeated quite often these days, and it may happen here too. This is the way it goes with crypto crime. There is a certainty that by the time this book is published there will be many more hacks and thefts on the boards.

And so it gets its own chapter.

There is a crypto news outlet whose website I occasionally visit. It is called *rekt*. A phonetic spelling of *wrecked*. Its primary purpose is to report on the major hacks and thefts in the crypto space. They have a leader board on their site. It only goes back a couple of years, presumably when they started their news outlet. There have been somewhere north of 100 hacks since their first report in Q3 2020. This fits well with the explosion of Defi, where there were hundreds of products quickly rushed to market, probably with little testing. Each hack/theft is listed, along with some reporting about how it happened and how much was stolen.

It is a weird sort of vicarious joy to read these reports. Which is an entirely inappropriate reaction, I am aware. Perhaps it is the old-style typewriter font and graphics-free treatment. Perhaps it is the sheer breadth of different types of hacks recorded, across multiple types and genres of crypto projects. All of them violence against ownership which was not properly secured by crypto. Not yet, anyway. We are still young and reckless.

But there are a couple of moles worth whacking in the whole screechy, outraged headline-grabbing, regulator-point-scoring cacophony of the crypto-crime narrative.

There are three major genres of grift in the crypto space. The first is the wheelhouse of the unvarnished black-hat hacker thieves that gain illicit access to blockchain accounts and help themselves to tokens; the second are projects started by developers and/or marketers who attract capital for their 'projects' but at some point vanish with the funds (called rug pulls); and the third is a somewhat lesser grift, those use deceit and misinformation like 'pump and dump' to gain unfair advantage.

But before we take a look at these, let's understand how big the crypto crime industry really is.

What makes the BNB theft remarkable is its size. To suck out that much in a few minutes is a startling event, although obviously $560 million in crypto can be stolen in not much more time than $56, given the digital nature of things. There have actually been two larger heists than this – Ronin Network at $624 million and the Poly Network at $611 million. But it should be put in context.

About $50 billion, give or take, has been stolen or otherwise misappropriated in the decade and a half since Bitcoin kicked off in 2009. Compare that to various estimates that peg real-world financial fraud at $1.5 trillion *per year*, or nearly $20 trillion since 2009 (this is extrapolated from an Refinitiv. com survey entitled 'Revealing the True Cost of Financial Crime'[45]). $50 billion is insignificant next to that. More to the point – all crypto crime is visible – anyone can see it on the blockchain, even as it is unfolding in real time. But only a percentage of the real-world of financial crime even comes to light, so the $20 trillion figure is certain to be understated.

Chainalysis, the largest blockchain data forensics company in the world, estimates that only 0.15% of blockchain transactions are for illicit purposes, compared with 5% in the non-crypto world. So given both its quantum and the percentage of illicit transactions, I would claim that crime on the blockchain is rare compared to the more kleptocratic physical world in which we live. And I am not counting here the quiet squirrelling away of illegal money in Panamanian bank accounts or the wastage of tender inflation and overpricing. Most of which never sees the sunlight of justice.

Then there is the issue of visibility. Crypto crimes happen under the spotlight – it is entirely public, blockchain are open for viewing. As is where the stolen cryptotokens are stashed. They end up in wallets where everyone can see them. There are some clever laundering techniques deep in the cryptosphere, but companies like Chainalysis and Elliptic are paid fine bounties by the FBI and their ilk to keep track. It requires great skill to get away with crypto malfeasance. It is, in fact, far easier to steal in the fiat world.

But do I protest too much? Perhaps. There is a public perception of the cryptosphere as a free-for-all grab-what-you-can larceny, and it is quite difficult to change that perception by mere facts. So perhaps the answer lies in hardening security instead, which will reduce the instances of theft.

It turns out that *none* of the major blockchains have ever been hacked directly. Well almost. Bitcoin has never been hacked. In June 2016 an Ethereum was hacked via a buggy smart contract and was forced to modify the network in response, which was an ideological no-no, but they did. Herewith the story, recounted in the book *Beyond Bitcoin: Decentralised Finance and the End of Banks,* by me and co-writer Simon Dingle.

One of the most famous early projects in this space was The DAO, which was launched via ICO on April 30, 2016. Their big idea was that The DAO was to be a 'Decentralised Autonomous Organisation' by the very nature of its architecture. It was simply an organisation, but with no head and a flat democracy. Their plan was to raise money through the ICO, and then to have its token holders decide where and how to spend it. A sort of decentralised VC fund. No

CEO, no managers, just token holders voting on spend submissions. This was an intriguing idea, one that had been long discussed. Centralised payment and value transfer was all very well, but what about decentralised governance? A big idea, even very big, if you consider its possible use in democratic governments.

Sadly, the second reason for The DAO's fame, or more accurately notoriety, was that it got hacked. Over $50m worth (from $150m raised at its ICO). It was an enormous blow to the entire community, and particularly Ethereum, on which The DAO was built. It resulted in no less of an extreme reaction by Ethereum than a 'hard fork', which was essentially a new version of Ethereum, which included a patch of their core code, and an effective return of funds to those who had lost out. This was not the way things were supposed to work. Blockchains were supposed to be immutable. But the hard fork decision was taken, criticism was levelled far and wide, and the world continued.

In any event all the major hacks now are committed in the onion layers surrounding the blockchain. Some examples:

• Passwords/private keys have been inadvertently revealed (or via social hacking or plain foolishness). No one hacked the blockchain in these cases – they just used a purloined key to walk in. There has long been a plea for users to keep their own keys offline, and entrust them to no one, not even a reputable exchange. But people simply do not want to do that, because complexity intrudes again. So custody companies have sprung up, offering to take custody of keys. Meaning centralized trust, an anathema to the entire crypto ethos. Oh well.

- Smart contracts often have bugs. That is a fact of software life. Code is developed by humans and humans are not gods. There is a vibrant and profitable industry of companies staffed by rocket scientists who will test and certify smart contracts, but they are not gods either. A bad actor who finds the right bug can exploit it before it is found and snuffed out.
- There are now many other blockchains besides Bitcoin and Ethereum. And there are projects that have created 'bridges' between them. Many of the newer hacks have been on the bridges, where the short journey across the bridge is not as secure as the blockchains that protect the land on either side of the bridge.
- Centralized exchanges that take custody of user keys have had their key stores compromised.
- A slew of arcane technical hacks – API injections, flash loan attacks and others.

The actual criminal toolset is certainly bigger than this, but the message is that the kernel of modern crypto, the blockchain core code which assembles blocks of transactions, executes transfers and orchestrates the verification of transactions is diamond-hard, likely more so than any network in history. Although this is somewhat like saying that your house is extremely secure with beams and cameras and steel doors and barred windows and alarms. But then leaving your house keys in the custody of a stranger in a bar. Or worse, letting some rando workers picked up off the street into the house to paint it and leaving them unattended while you go out for a few hours.

There are a number of interesting nuances in the grift landscape. The 2022 Crypto Crime Report by Chainalysis[46] traverses them. Bad actors who know software at a deep level are obviously a dangerous group, they are in possession of rare technical skills, and they are often funded by rogue states. Expert lock-pickers would be the real-life analogy. But then there are the straight-up scamsters, who prey on the gullible, unsuspecting, naive or foolishly optimistic. The best analogy for these criminals are like the tricksters of the street-level Three-card Monte variety, except that much more is at stake under the cups.

The increase in crypto crime from 2020 to 2021 was marked, from about $7 billion to $14 billion and 2022 looks to be even worse. And the biggest increase came from the scammers rather than the software hackers – about 80% up from 2020. Scamming is a different sort of headwind than hacks – more a consequence of lax regulation and credulous innocents rather than being a systemic flaw in crypto armour. Scammers will always be there, particularly in the sort of world where fortunes can be made quickly, an unfortunate fact of the cryptoverse, at least up until 2022.

But so pervasive and inventive have bad guys been in finding chinks in layers surrounding the core, that there is now a great deal of energy being poured into shoring up those defences. The non-crypto online world had its share of barbarians at the gate too – DDos attacks, ransomware, phishing malware and authentic-looking but deceitful come-ons and redirects. It will likely never end, just as we will never clean our physical world of bad actors. It is the price we pay in a world where virtue is not all-encompassing and in which there will always be someone on the side of vice.

So, yes, the headlines and headwinds of crypto-crime will remain, but as the blockchain seeps into all of our lives over the next decade perhaps they will subside somewhat, and become the dissonant and constant background hum along with all other financial misdeeds.

In the earlier chapter on the mathematics of secrets I offered an analogy of secret-keeping by describing a standard lockbox in which some family heirlooms are stored. There were some fairly obvious requirements for ownership of the contents to be considered safe.

The key should be safely secured in a hiding place that should be minimally shared (or ideally not shared at all), the key should actually open the box, the locking mechanism should not be broken or breakable. In the grifts, scams and hacks indicated above, keys are handed over to bad actors, locks get broken, owners are tricked into putting their heirlooms into wrong boxes, owners are tricked into revealing the keys' hiding places, and so on, even if the box itself is a secure container. Not a perfect analogy to be sure, but it illustrates where the vulnerabilities in the crypto ecosystem lie. The new forms of ownership described in this book will start to approach their full potential and benefit as each of these soft spots is hardened and secured by the growing intellectual power being deployed to this problem.

* * *

I want to end this chapter with a remarkable story. It fits squarely in-between a grift and a genius trade. I am not totally sure of where the moral line lies.

On 11th October 2022, a guy and his team helped themselves to $114 million, not only keeping $47 million of it without threat of legal action, but also going public, doxxing himself and saying – *yeah, it was me, have a nice day.*

At the core of this story lies the subtle difference between the definition of a hack and an exploit. For instance, a hacker who breaks into crypto and steals cryptocurrency using a purloined private key is a thief, a robber, a breaker-and-enterer and a criminal. There are legions of these crimes across the crypto space. The perp or perps are always anonymous – they do not want to get caught, because they will go to jail. Which sometimes happens, although not often enough.

Then there is another sort of play. I am not sure whether to call it a scam, a grift or a crime or just good trading, it does not really fit neatly into any of those definitions. What happened to Mango Markets on 11th October is a perfect example.

Mango Markets is a crypto project that facilitates lending and borrowing and margin trading in the crypto markets. There are a number of similar projects in this space, they deliver an important service to the crypto economy. Mango and similar projects all leverage a core advantage of block-chain – the ability for a piece of software, called a smart contract, to replace the function of the bank or exchange or other financial middlemen.

Mango Markets is not a fly-by-night. The amount of value that they manage has reached as high as $200 million, dropping to about $150 million as world markets have crashed. And then one day $114 million disappeared from their coffers.

What generally happens in these cases is that the developers, aided by an army of Good Samaritan developers out in the world, dive in to try to find out what happened. Smart contracts are open-source code, anyone can see them – internal project developers… and outsiders, both good and bad. In any event,

241

they found a bug in the code. Or more accurately an extremely subtle vulnerability in the way the application operates, which no one else had spotted since its release years before.

Except a guy called Avraham Eisenberg. Eisenberg is not a black-hat hacker wearing a dark hoodie, he has posted for years on various blogs like Substack, explaining how he and his team study Defi protocols and find ways to trade profitably. He has explained his techniques without hiding them. There is a 24th January Substack post entitled – 'How our team makes millions in crypto risk-free'. The article goes into detail on how he does it. All above board, doing what armies of traders and hedge funds try to do in the real world.

All of this netted him a few per cent per week in profits, sometimes more. An enormous amount if you look at the annual take. But nothing compared to his $114 million haul at Mango.

The details of how he did this trade are less important than this – he did not hack Mango. He simply found a way to use its rules and process to leverage out the money. Nothing illegal at all. The Mango Market smart contract was not supposed to enable this sort of trade. But it did, and he saw it and simply played by its rules.

Here is what he said on a Twitter thread when he doxxed himself a few days after the hack on 14th October.

I was involved with a team that operated a highly profitable trading strategy last week.

I believe all of our actions were legal open market actions, using the protocol as designed, even if the development team did not fully anticipate all the consequences of setting parameters the way they are.

Unfortunately, the exchange this took place on, Mango Markets, became insolvent as a result, with the insurance fund being insufficient to cover all liquidations. This led to other users being unable to access their funds.

To remedy the situation, I helped negotiate a settlement agreement with the insurance fund with the goal of making all users whole as soon as possible as well as recapitalizing the exchange.

As a result of this agreement, once the Mango team finishes processing, all users will be able to access their deposits in full with no loss of funds.[47]

It was a little stranger than that. Because Mango Markets offers its token-holders (kind of like stockholders) the opportunity to submit proposals for improvements in the system, Eisenberg, who obviously held many tokens, submitted a proposal that said (I paraphrase here), 'Hi everyone. I will return everything but $47 million. That way your insurance fund will cover everyone, and no one loses money. And oh, you must indemnify me from legal action.'

The community voted 97% in favour. So he walked away with his money and indemnification. The $47 million was called a 'bug bounty' – a reward for finding a flaw in the system.

For a while it looked at though he would walk into the sunset with his loot, but in January of 2023 he was arrested in Puerto Rico and criminally charged by the SEC. The case is now making its way through the courts.

He might win, convince a judge that he simply used the project as intended, played by the rules. If so, the blame lies squarely with the architects of the smart contract who let some smarter smarty-pants outsmart them.

Chapter 20

WHY TOKEN?

We have made a case in this book that it is the prospect of a new way of encoding ownership that is the fuel powering blockchain's horizontal spread across every discipline and industry. And while we have spent some time looking at the ownership dynamics of cryptocurrencies and NFTs and the other related projects that have coalesced around them, it is worth stepping up one layer of abstraction and talk about that which turns the engines of ownership economies and attaches value to them.

The token.

The subject of tokens and the economics rules under which they operate (called tokenomics) is often misunderstood, partially because blockchains do not *require* tokens. For instance, IBM's Fabric is a non-token emitting blockchain, as are others, like Corda's R3. In fact, the marketing materials for these products describe themselves as distributed ledger technologies rather than blockchains, presumably to put some daylight between them and the grubby world of public blockchains and their tokens.

Consider a simple blockchain that has a single use – to securely store university credentials. The credentials of a particular graduate can be viewed by anyone who knows the public key, but can only be lodged and modified by the university, which holds the private key for each graduate's address on the blockchain. This is not a particularly good use of blockchain, given the trust is centralized and delegated to someone in the university, and could probably more easily implemented using any fairly modern non-blockchain tech stack with appropriate security – but be that as it may, tokens are convenient mechanism for crypto projects, but not a necessity.

So why are they employed? Because tokens are most often used as the grease of incentive to nudge stakeholders to behave in a certain way, as well as being a simple mechanism to facilitate transfer of ownership or control of the underlying digital value. The word 'value' should not be construed as financial value; it is much broader as we shall see. But first, a trip into various thesauri (again) yielded some insight. Consider this definition, from Dictionary.com:

something serving to represent or indicate some fact...; a characteristic indication or mark of something; evidence or proof;

I'll take some licence and meld these two together – *a crypto-token is evidence or proof of some fact*. It is indeed a proof of ownership of something. But this statement understates the wider implications, so let's spread some examples on the table to bring it into focus.

Whether we choose to act on it or not, ownership of something always has value attached, for someone. We own things we may want to sell now, or later, to a willing buyer. We own things that we would never dream of selling, at any price. We own things we may want to give away. We also own things that have value to us, but no one else. The tokens emitted by blockchain projects are all owned representations of something with underlying value. The near-instantaneous success of the Bitcoin blockchain, with its similarly named Bitcoin token, has served to muddy the waters, leaving most people to believe that cryptotokens are all currencies whose value is determined in an open and public market, but there are many other kinds of tokens where ownership and value and usage and ecosystems are entangled differently and surprisingly across multiple axes.

A lovely example of this can be found in the BAT token (Basic Attention Token). There is a popular Internet browser called Brave. It looks rather like Chrome but it is privacy-focused, not sharing its user's information with advertisers, as does Chrome. However, users of Brave may choose, at their discretion, to pay attention to certain ads, and will get paid in BAT tokens as a reward. Brave then shares revenue from these ads to those people who 'paid attention' to them. The user of the Brave browser obviously owns the time they spend on reading an ad. Brave values that time spent. It both shares revenue with the user and awards BAT tokens, which are tradable on the open market, the appreciation driven, presumably, by more and more people signing up to BAT rewards, and so driving more and more revenue to Brave via its users' attention to online ads, and so drive up the value of the token.

The BAT token gives indirect ownership of a revenue stream that is fuelled by user attention to advertising. Very meta and very cool.

A paper in a journal called 'Blockchain: Research and Applications' (Pierluigi Freni et al.) builds a matrix that seeks to taxonomize different ways that tokens express themselves to their holders and the ecosystems in which they live. To give an example of the depth and breadth of the thinking around this, the authors identify tokens that enable the right to work, or right to use, or right to vote, or as a unit of account, or a medium of exchange, or a store of value. Another column offers the following possible incentives that could apply to the enabling tokens – get access, get discount, get reward, get revenue, dividend potential, appreciation potential, governance participation, reputation gain.

And those are only two columns in the matrix. There are fourteen columns in total. Forty-two options. To give an example, Bitcoin checks the following boxes in the matrix (I will truncate, for mercy's sake):

- Incentive Drivers: Appreciation
- Incentive Enablers: Unit of account, medium of exchange, store of value
- Supply Strategy: Schedule-based
- Underlying Value: Network-value
- Tradability: Tradable
- Divisibility: Fractional
- Fungibility: Fungible
- Expirability: Non-expirable

And so on. This may look like a wonky and exhaustive academic exercise deep in the weeds of taxonomy design, but it reveals a fundamentally important point. It is that ownership is value-attracting, fuelled by incentives, driven by behaviours, supported by technology. Again, Eula Biss's *'giant vessel' of ownership* looms, and in the case of blockchain and tokens and the Freni taxonomy, sliced into digestible boxes, as befits its digital form, which can manifest and interact in myriad forms.

Which leads to a challenge, and it is a challenge of trust. When someone sells you or awards you a cryptotoken, how do you determine precisely what it is and what the conditions of that ownership implies? In the case of Bitcoin, it is fairly simple. You own a token. It has a certain value on public markets. You can store it or use it to buy things from anyone who will take it as payment. Or you can simply hold it and hope for appreciation. There will never be more than 21 million of them, the last one minted in 2140. Wait! Did you know that last one? I suspect the vast majority of Bitcoin holders don't. They do not really understand the deeper dynamics of the token that they hold in their crypto wallet. And Bitcoin is an extremely simple case.

It gets even more opaque if there is an underlying smart contract which controls the token's movements under various conditions. So now the token owner needs to understand the behaviour of the token and how it may be manipulated and moved by the underlying smart contract. At least if the owner is to be fully informed.

It is not quite as scary as it seems. No one reads the fine print in the real world either, which are likely buried in impossible terms and conditions somewhere. An obvious example – how many of the millions of shareholders of Apple have read the shareholder's agreement? But in the cryptoverse the ideologues who populate its territory have a leg up. Many of them are obsessive about finding unfairness and spend much free time crawling around the cryptoverse finding boils and publicly lancing them on social media. Leaving the non-technical user with a public trail of information to find on

Google, which is somewhat better than asking a lawyer to explain a multi-hundred page shareholder agreement from Apple.

Let's then disentangle the ownership web again. The token itself is owned by the holder of the private key. It may be fungible or non-fungible, or a right to vote, or a right of entry, or a currency, or contain any of the other cogs as stated by the taxonomy described earlier (there are other taxonomies; this one will suffice for our needs). Tokens are either 'native' to a blockchain like Bitcoin, or are under control of a smart contract, as are the many cryptotokens hosted on the Ethereum blockchain. In the latter case the user is at a disadvantage, needing either deep knowledge or trust (or both) to fully understand the terms of ownership. Given that smart contracts are programs, and can be arbitrarily complex, this is a tall order for almost all holders, who must now rely on knowledgeable actors in the crypto community to understand and explain and vouch for tokens on public forums like Twitter.

So let us draw this to a close by offering you this:

a token is a unit of account, representing an underlying value, which is determined by software that seeks to influence token holders' behaviours towards a goal set by the token designers

Or if you prefer, in more formal language of Freni et al.:

a token can be intended as a socio-economic tool to promote the coordination of the actors in a regulated ecosystem towards the pursuit of a network objective function through a set of incentive systems.[48]

And finally, the reason I am making a meal of this is to offer a health warning. Ownership brings with it responsibility. And while we can be sure that our ownership is safely secured by underlying mathematics, as owners we still are burdened with the requirement to understand the terms and conditions of that ownership, whether they are written by a lawyer or coded by a developer.

Chapter 21

RWA – THE GIANT HYBRID BABY

On 23rd August 2018, a press release was distributed by the World Bank. It announced that they had issued the first global bond on a blockchain. It was nicknamed Bond-*i* (blockchain operated new debt instrument). It was arranged by the Commonwealth Bank of Australia and purchased by numerous blue-chip financial institutions. $110 million was raised, with demand outstripping supply.

No one outside of a small cadre of finance and crypto wonks thought much about it, other than as a curious experiment, but it was perhaps the official start of what is now expected to be a $16 trillion industry by 2030 (BCG),[49] a massive number that would overwhelm all other sectors in crypto and rewire the issuance of legacy capital markets.

How did this all come together?

While tokenization has been embedded in blockchain applications from the start, it was only in about 2017, a few years after Ethereum's release, that a few observant and forward-thinking mandarins of traditional high finance drew a now-obvious connection from the world of crypto to their world – the world of capital markets where complex and many-layered assets are packaged and issued to investors to fund all manner of global commerce.

Capital markets and the private debt and equity that they fund are a massive institutional business, now worth over $120 trillion per year,[50] globally diverse and largely out of the public eye. This business is not sexy, has been around for hundreds of years, and usually moves not much faster the speed of creakily architected legacy systems from the 1990s. Months are required to package a product, issue it, secure it, record it, distribute it, document it and close the investment. It is well understood by its participants and it provides attractive risk-mitigated yields unavailable to the rest of us.

And so I imagine one of these mandarins from 2017/2018 said: Wait a minute! Tokens on the blockchain can be securely owned and can move around in near real time and be tracked and traced and measured with certainty and immutability. If we legally tether tokens to our gnarly and complex financial assets all manner of magic will happen. Like access to a wider investor market and therefore easier access to capital! Speed of settlement! Reduction of middlemen! Simplicity of process! And so Bond-*i* arrived, apparently after a year of careful work, quietly opening what has now become a floodgate.

The sector that has grown up in the wake of the World Bank bond is called tokenized real-world assets, or its more uninspired nickname RWA. Tokens, as we have seen, can be tethered to anything, real or virtual. And it seems that the world of big finance has woken up the obvious, particularly in the past year.

And so now there is this hot corner of the usually very public world of crypto in which innovation is quietly crackling and popping, with hundreds of millions of dollars already moving to and fro on a near-daily basis, with none of it ending up on the front pages of the media.

Here is what is going on under the hood:

Somewhere behind the stern facades of all financial institutions is a well-worn set of machinery that provides financial services, usually in the form of loans, to enable the building, manufacturing, moving, distributing, beneficiation, buying, selling, trading of all the stuff that we, as citizens, end up consuming and using. The money required for a shipment of cars from China to Australia. The loan to cover the gap between and the sending of a large invoice and the payment and settlement of that invoice. The loan to build an Italian manufacturing plant in Vietnam.

These high-finance products are beasts. Hundreds of pages of documentation and legalese. Statutory and compliance requirements. The machine that makes this all happen is attended by many actors, stakeholders and bit players – producers, shippers, distributors, retailers, customs officials, lawyers, brokers, handlers, fixers, regulators, port authorities and, of course, capital providers whose money greases the many wheels along the way. These many actors strut their stuff and then look to get paid for their labours. So that fuel ends up in the aircraft we are flying or the food that ends up in our stomachs.

If one looks under the hood, there are often ten, twenty, thirty or even more players along the chain of events, sometimes acting in sequence and sometimes in parallel. It has been that way for a long time; a set of hardened and inflexible processes that ultimately supply superior yield for a protected few.

But it is this grindy, gnarly, complex set of cogs and wheels that makes commerce chunk away without most people noticing. Until something doesn't arrive on our doorstep or on the shelf at our local shop or in the medicine storage facility at the hospital when our child is awaiting a critical procedure. Then we notice. Loudly and pissed-offedly.

It is hellishly complex. I know – I tried to understand the supply chain of a fleet of cars being ordered from one country to another. It left me aghast and thankful that I had chosen a simpler career.

So the first realization of the early adopters was that that the blockchain could be used to flatten the layers of process, instantly removing mountains of friction facing participants on all sides of the market.

But there was more. There is about $160 billion in stablecoins currently residing in various wallets and pools across the crypto space. Much of it unused, belonging to owners biding their time until opportunity knocks. The price of these stablecoins is, well, stable – no wild volatility here. But all these stablecoin owners would dearly love to attract some fine yields, provided risks are low. And where you have projects looking for capital and lots of capital available, there is a conversation to be had. There are many of these projects (like trade finance) that are indeed low-risk, well-understood, process-hardened. Clearly a Goldman Sachs-arranged real-world loan would be preferable than a stablecoin owner throwing the dice on another hot new untested crypto project. If only the stablecoin owner had a way to buy the real-world loan...

But because one side of this business lives in the traditional world, and the other in the crypto world, there has always been mostly silence between them, with different languages and cultures preventing much cross-talk. That is changing quickly, the potential rewards crumbling any resistance. A common language is emerging.

Before we get too excited here, a caveat.

The complexities of supply chain, trade finance and other 'alternative' assets remain as labyrinthine as ever. The thick pile of asset and issuance documents and compliance does not simply disappear. But RWA innovation is not trying to side-step the embedded statutories. It is about how to use tokenization to lighten the load, to move transaction data quickly, to lock down certainty and security of ownership. And how to make it easy and fast and efficient for old-world financiers to access underutilized crypto capital. And as importantly, how to democratize access to large low-risk institutional finance deals for small investors, even down to retail peons like me, who would otherwise have no chance to get a piece of these arcane instruments, previously only accessible to the upper layers of the financial hierarchy that most of us never see (or even know exists).

So companies are pouring into the space – names like Goldfinch, Truefi, Maple, Ondo, Centrifuge, Aave, MakerDAO. To say nothing of internal projects moving from small proofs-of-concept to production rollouts in the bowels of the big global financial institutions – JP Morgan, Sovereign Bank of Singapore, Société Générale.

How is it going so far, this new baby? $4 billion total loans, nearly 1,600 active loans, average of more than 13% return for the stablecoin lenders (this last figure is probably unsustainable at that rate, but still). And this is just the retail-facing numbers, and does not include the private financing between institutions, like World Bank's Bond-i. This time next year? I am going with a prediction of a 10x increase in RWA activity.

Crypto loans collateralized by solid real-word things – a marriage of opposites. Which will also feed the appetite of new investors coming into the crypto space to seize this new day.

Creating a virtuous circle.

Perhaps exactly the circle everyone in this field has been waiting for, even as we averted our eyes from the toxicity of hackers, barkers, maxis and grifters that have for too long captured the news cycle.

Chapter 22

WHERE IS ALL OF THIS HEADED?

There is a temptation, especially as this author brings his narrative to closure, to say, 'And therefore…'

There can be no such luxury. If one ignores the ownership implications that we have talked about and just looks at what has shaken out of this blockchain tree in the mere thirteen years of its life, it is evident that predictions, or at least specific predictions, are a fool's game. No one saw the conspiracy of mathematics, cryptography, software, applied technology, communications, networking, consensus algorithms, finance, payments, economics, culture, art, sociology, psychology, democracy, law, decentralization, politics, game theory, history, hacks, bugs, collaboration, enthusiasm and emotion converging so quickly and with so little planning and with so many intended and unintended consequences.

I went to Google Scholar and nosed around a bit. Who was studying this stuff and in what disciplines? Here is a smattering:

- Tokenization: The Key to Philosophy, Physics, and Psychology (Yardley)
- Toward a Political Sociology of Blockchain (Jones)
- Blockchain and law: Incompatible codes? (Millard)

- The economics of crypto-democracy (Berg et al.)
- Anthropology and blockchain (Komarski et al.)
- The political imaginaries of blockchain projects: discerning the expressions of an emerging ecosystem (Husein et al.).
- Cryptoeconomics: Designing effective incentives and governance models for blockchain networks using insights from economics (Barrera et al.)
- Blockchain token economics: A mean-field-type game perspective (Barreiro-Gome et al.)
- A novel decision-making model with Pythagorean fuzzy linguistic information measures and its application to a sustainable blockchain product assessment problem (Jin et al.)
- A Blockchain-based Application as Part of a Digital Diplomacy Approach to Facilitate and Advance Cyber Diplomacy (Ce Cirnu et al.)

And on. And on. You get the point. If you look across the entire spectrum of academic, investigation, research and pedagogy you will find that cryptography and blockchain are seeping into genres of fundamental research everywhere, including into nooks and crannies very far from the hue and cry of money and markets. And I am ignoring the industry verticals like health and supply chain and energy and education where there are new blockchain applications rolled out continuously.

So I tumbled into the analytics, as I do occasionally, to seek answers as to how far and wide this blockchain industry is spreading and how that is supported in the numbers. But the data that has exploded out of the crypto firehouse since 2009 is unquenchable and undigestible. Across every metric imaginable, not just the obvious price movements of digital assets on public markets. Entire billion-dollar businesses have sprung up from nowhere whose entire *raison-d'être* is to make sense of all the multidimensional data surrounding the industry – Chainalysis, Elliptical, Glassnode, Messari, Nansen, not to mention the traditional providers of industry reports, like PWC and Accenture who seek to take a wider view. Taking a peek into these sources is, well, blinding. There seems to simply be too much data to make sense of the gestalt of industry, at least concerning what there is to be learned about *exactly* where it is going in the future, save for direction.

So instead of rattling off a bunch of mostly unconnected statistics about its growth, I am going to deliver just one startling fact.

Stanford University has long been the uncontested king of computer science education. It sits squarely in Silicon Valley and the number of applications for its freshman year 'Introduction to Computer Science' is by far the most over-subscribed, and is the most popular course offered by the institution. Has been for over twenty years. In the autumn of 2022, it was overtaken in number of applicants and popularity for the first time by another freshman course.

The name of the course is 'Introduction to Blockchain'. (Although I suspect that 'An Introduction to AI' might soon wear this mantle; another equally transformative new technology exploding all around us as this book goes to final print.)

Why is this? One could be cynical and assume that these and other blockchain classes that are beginning to sprout up at every major university are filled to the brim with single-minded young wealth-seekers, given the rapid value creation that we have seen over the past thirteen years. That may be partially true, or true for some, as it was when the Internet took off in the late 1990s and early noughts, with universities spewing out techies and economists and marketers and designers, all looking to swim somewhere in its rising tides.

But it is also true that many young people coming into the tertiary education system are interested in ideas rather than careers, or if they wish, both. I know a couple of them quite well – young relatives and some of their friends. In the halcyon days of easy money some of these then teenagers, most still in high school, certainly became enamoured of the opportunity for a quick buck. And some even learned how to mint NFTs, when that became a thing, hoping, perhaps to be the next Beeple, or at least to make enough to buy new Nikes.

But the fast-money aspect of crypto has now been diluted somewhat, and something else seems to be at play as these young adults enter or continue their tertiary studies, even if it might not be clearly understood. And I believe it is the osmosis of opinion and worldviews of social media. For anyone who spends any time there, there are libraries of content around crypto and blockchain, aside from the usual barking and inanity. Unlike many other industries, a good portion of deep crypto thinking happens on Twitter and YouTube and podcasts. Here, I am talking about those who carefully analyse, ruminate and consider what all of this crypto-fuelled innovation means and where it is taking us.

But I am a fairly recent convert to the crypto-wisdom available to any one determined enough to mine the deep and rich veins that can be found on Twitter. I expect that the many young people clamouring for education in this space are not recent converts – social media is where they have grown up.

In my most optimistic moments I would like to believe that many young people flocking to find out about blockchain are doing so because of what it represents, rather than the pockets it may line.

* * *

One of the people I recently discovered as I started to follow the best of social media thinking was Josh Rosenthal (@JoshuaRosenthal), who popped onto my radar recently. Not a youngster, but a wise social media luminary nevertheless.

He is a PhD, Fulbright Scholar, Harvard guest lecturer, polymath sort of guy – history, health science, public policy, data analytics, crypto. You know, an all-rounder genius. But what really strikes me about Dr Rosenthal (his demeanour makes it likely that he hates being called that), is his ability to structure an unbroken seven-minute answer to a ten-second question – expertly pitched, well-structured, narratively arced to perfection. His appearances on YouTube are small gems of performance.

Here is his thesis: Rosenthal has a specific interest in the Renaissance. He describes the accretion of power that had sclerotized in the hundreds and thousands of years before the 1500s. Nation-states, monarchies, religions, master-serf relationships – impregnable towers undisturbed for generations.

And then... the Gutenberg press and the double-entry accounting system – both marvels of human ingenuity and both deeply disruptive.

When most people think of the Gutenberg Press they think Bibles. Nuh-uh. The low-brow consequences were much more important. Cartoons. Graphics. Memes! It showed people that other lives, other thoughts, other worldviews, were out there begging to be explored. It was the start of the decentralization of the common man's hopes and dreams.

And as for double-entry accounting – suddenly debits and credits were tethered together in a mutual embrace. It changed commerce and the measurement of business.

Ideas and matters of exchange had quickly morphed into a cornucopia of options, pushing aside the monochrome constraints of the past.

Rosenthal is at great pains to point out the Renaissance did not suddenly appear. There were lots of little revolutions, false starts and tentative pushbacks to long-entrenched authority. That is, until the new ideas convincingly won, fuelling 500 or so years of massive human change – political, societal, economic, commercial and technological.

But quietly and determinedly, as Rosenthal points out, new accretions of power have begun to assemble themselves again. Political superpowers. Business monoliths. Oligarchs. Myopic information factories. And distribution monopolies like Facebook, Google and Twitter.

Here is where Rosenthal sees all this urgent innovation bubbling out of the crypto waters and hears the rhymes of the Renaissance. New ways to own stuff, new ways to take and keep possession, new ways to resist the surveillance of the state, new ways to thwart censorship and avoid theft. New ways to form communities of like purpose. And new ways to subvert the tendency of power to centralize around a small elite.

Once Rosenthal starts to draw parallels between that Renaissance and what is happening now, it is hard not to see the similarities everywhere. The continuous spawning of new experiments across multiple axes of human activity, the pushback of regulators and states, the outrage of big media, the gradual signs of capitulation and floor crossing among the common man.

Rosenthal's view of what is really happening here may sound hyperbolic — A NEW RENAISSANCE! But he is not some schmuck infected by that old hoary 'irrational enthusiasm' chestnut. Any cursory perusing of his deeper analyses is convincing by dint of his analysis. It is not hyperbolic at all. It is much more important than that.

I like to think that some fifteen-year-old somewhere watched Rosenthal on YouTube and said, 'Hmm – I want to go to Stanford and study blockchain one day.'

* * *

Chris Dixon is a General Partner at the Andreessen Horowitz (or a16z as it is better known). It is the world's largest venture investor in blockchain and crypto initiatives, and it is the area that Dixon leads. He is also one of the better known 'crypto-philosophers' at a16z, famous for constructing conceptual models for thinking about crypto and its many parts.

I came upon a 2021 tweet of his which was arresting, because it shed yet another light on the ownership story, one quite removed from the ownership story in this book.

He tweeted: 'Blockchains are special computers that anyone can access but no one owns.'

The thinking behind this statement bears comment. Dixon and colleagues have formulated an approach to blockchain that starts here – the blockchain is a special type of computer architecture that, for the first time in computer history, makes software the master of hardware, rather than the other way around.

The hierarchy has always been this – owner of hardware first, then hardware, then software. Software can always be disabled by pulling the plug on hardware, and the only ones who can pull the plug on hardware are its owners. Software is subservient to and dependent on hardware and its owners. He gives a comparison between a hypothetical Googlecoin and Bitcoin. If Google owns the hardware that runs the software that operates Googlecoin, they are therefore the arbiters of the software, just as they are the arbiters of Chrome OS. They can change, censor or remove software at their discretion, because the software is a slave in the relationship.

In the case of Bitcoin or Ethereum, this is not possible. The entire architecture of the system is inverted. The software incentivizes the owners of the hardware (the validators or miners) *not* to pull the plug. There are many of these computers running the software, and it is in no one's economic interest to arbitrarily stop doing so en masse, because of those economic incentives. Moreover, this architecture has another dimension, and that is that the computer can be trusted to *commit*. The software cannot be arbitrarily changed, unless in agreement by all parties who participate in its economic and technical ecosystem. This was true of 2022's Merge in the Ethereum ecosystem, which moved it to a less energy-intensive consensus mechanism – all validator nodes were consulted, and a vote taken for the change.

This may seem like deep-in-the-weeds philosophical musings, but it is not. This is the first fundamental change to computer architecture since the famed 1945 'Von Neumann' computer architecture, taught to all computer science graduates and the basis for nearly all computers in existence.

It is the first sighting of this new architecture since the birth of computing – it is an ownership story reversed, and will require the benefit of hindsight to fully understand its implications. But Dixon and colleagues are certain enough to have raised over $6 billion to back their wager, and their website is brimming with conversations about the implications of this architectural change. Given their track record, I wouldn't bet against them.

There are a number of other threads that unspool from the 'where is all of this headed?' question.

One of them comes from another trope discussed at a16z called 'the blockchain space market'. In short, all these blockchains launching and optimizing their innards and competing for transactions will eventually result in a glut of blockspace. Lots of blocks looking to be filled with transactions or other blobs of trustless communication. Who will use this space, and for what? An analogy offered by a16z is broadband, and the glut of capacity that arrived as participants rushed into the space some years back. Many broadband companies found themselves over-capitalized and under pressure as they waited for customers. And then they arrived. Swarms of them. YouTube, Netflix, Disney, Apple TV, HBO, TikTok and a furious global migration from video broadcast to streaming. Very quickly the shortage of content to fill those pipes ended – entrepreneurs saw the empty infrastructure and found a way to use it profitably, along with new ways to sweat the infrastructure. The management at a16z sees this happening with blockspace too. Build it and they will come.

A second thread relates to blockchain competition. One of the axioms of blockchain is called the trilemma dilemma, posited by Vitalek Buterin. Blockchain architecture sits on three legs – security (tamper resistance), decentralization (censorship resistance) and scalability (throughput). The dilemma states that you can optimize for two of these legs, but not all three – there are intractable technical tensions between them. A consequence of this is that there will be blockchains that optimize for one combination or other of these legs, driven by the requirements of the applications that run on top of them. A security and privacy-focused application (like secure messaging) has entirely different requirements than a retail payment application which may have more need for fast throughput. Horses for courses – there will be many different blockchains differently tuned driven by application requirements.

A third thread relates to zero-knowledge proof that we briefly mentioned in the previous chapter. One of the facts of blockchain is that all participating nodes on the blockchain verify the same transactions – they run the same verification code. Zero-knowledge proofs raise the spectre of completely eliminating that burden from the network, which would supercharge speed of execution by orders of magnitude.

Those are only three threads. Obviously there are many others. And then a tapestry will emerge.

* * *

And finally there is this. The past few years has seen not only a rush of students entering this field, but a concomitant rush of experienced talent migrating from the erstwhile prestige of top tech companies into new blockchain projects. I did a Google search on this – the media is awash with tales of top talent from Facebook, Google, Meta and Microsoft turning their backs on successful careers and big salaries to join blockchain companies.

If you combine the migration of experienced professionals into the blockchain world with the overflowing classes in those universities that have started to offer blockchain curricula, it becomes evident that the intellectual and creative energy of the best of the best is looking to the field for fulfilment, creative succour, challenge, career and perhaps even meaning. This is no small matter. The coalescence of this amount of brain power, especially across multiple fields of human endeavour, from the purely scientific to the humanities, indicates to me that we are witnessing the birth of technology that is making claim to be amongst the transformative in human history.

I read a bunch of interviews from individuals who were shedding their old lives in tradtech, many of them comfortable, and who talked about 'why I am leaving for blockchain'. The reasons given were never dissatisfaction with the old tech, but excitement about the new.

One of these interviews jumped out at me. It was with Evan Cheng, a top engineer and tech leader at Facebook/Meta who left for the world of blockchain, starting a company called Mysten Labs.

He said, 'I've built a lot of technologies, there is nothing quite like this. It really, really changes how you can build products, and if you think about that the asset is in the hand of the keyholder, which could be the person himself, or a trusted third party, then you change the concept of ownership itself, of who owns the product and eliminating the middleman, changing the cost of everything in our daily lives.'

There you have it. *You change the concept of ownership itself.*

Epilogue

In the introduction to this book I mentioned that I had co-written a book called *Beyond Bitcoin: Decentralised Finance and the End of Banks* with Simon Dingle. We decided to write that book in early 2021, not long after Defi had burst into view like blazing Halloween fireworks, setting off a chain of experimentation which, while having roller-coastered with other global matters over the last few years, seems unbowed and full of kinetic energy as I write.

The core of this book – the tight tether between cryptography and ownership – took inchoate shape over the period that we researched, wrote and launched *Beyond Bitcoin*.

But it only snapped into focus in 2022 during the early stages of the Russian invasion of Ukraine, where citizens in both countries found themselves on the same side of wartime problem, no matter what their politics. Everyone wanted to protect whatever capital they could. Banks and their infrastructure were being destroyed, Russian citizens were cut off from Swift, currencies were under threat of immediate and massive devaluation. Citizens in both countries were staring financial ruin in the face (in addition to other obviously more life-threatening outcomes). And so many on both sides turned to cryptocurrencies, where they could safely transform their local wealth into something less risky than wartime currency. Once the currencies were migrated to Bitcoin or ETH or Tether or USDC they owned it. It was not subject to seizure or debasement in an uncertain future of inevitable economic ructions in both countries. For them the matter of private non-censorable ownership of value was a matter of survival, not merely an interesting new tech experiment. They could not trust that their governments would or could rebuild, nor could they trust the exigencies of global events to make them whole; the politics had spun too far out of control. They needed to take trust off the table and did. Futures were saved by the certainty and surety of blockchain value ownership.

I thought a lot about what I owned in the year that I spent writing this book, and how my assumptions had never been tested. I have lost stuff that I owned, and I have had stuff stolen; I have mentioned two of those experiences in this book. There were others. A laptop with an unfinished novel before cloud backup, many years ago. A driver's licence, requiring a visit to a municipal bureaucracy and a long wait in a queue. Another laptop, carelessly left at Sydney airport, never recovered. An iPhone, a catastrophe. Keys, daily. A spare tyre, stolen while I ate at a restaurant, the thief darting under the 4x4 where it hung and snipping a cable. A vaccination card. A near-mugging at an ATM. A credit card. A train ticket. A password, many times. Not all of these experiences would have been be helped by the blockchain (except potentially the driver's licence, vaccination cards and passwords) – other than a pathetic and somewhat comic claim to ownership and provenance, even though the item is gone forever.

But I also thought about my ownership of various crypto assets. Some cryptocurrency in a non-custodial wallet, some cryptocurrency in a centralized exchange, some nearly forgettable underperforming Defi tokens, and two low-value

NFTs. They make me happy, notwithstanding the crash. I know where my private keys are. This 'feels' different to other stuff I own. It 'feels' solid. Everything else in my life feels potentially unmoored, I can imagine scenarios where things I own can be snatched, lost, misplaced, seized. Even my house. It happens. Where there are people in charge, it happens. I would prefer maths to be in charge, at least for those things that need perfect predictability. Humans have many fine qualities, but perfect predictability is not one of them. That's what makes humans interesting.

But I would prefer the ownership of my possessions to be perfectly predictable, forever.

Endnotes

1 Eula Biss, *Having and Being Had* (Riverhead Books, 2020).
2 Tilman Hartley, 'The Continuing Evolution of Ownership'. *PLoS One*. 2019 Feb 12;14(2):e0211871. doi: 10.1371/journal.pone.0211871. PMID: 30753234; PMCID: PMC6372161
3 James Salzman and Michael Heller, *Mine! How the Hidden Rules of Ownership Control Our Lives* (Doubleday 2021).
4 Simon Singh, *The Code Book: The Science of Secrecy from Ancient Egypt to Quantum Cryptography* (Random House, 1999).
5 David Kahn, *The Story of Secret Writing* (Macmillan 1967).
6 Kathryn Judge, *Direct: The Rise of the Middleman Economy and the Power of Going to the Source* (HarperCollins 2022).
7 Overview of Trustee Corporations Industry, www.fsc.org.au.
8 Venkata Marella, Bikesh Upreti, Jani Merikivi et al, 'Understanding the creation of trust in cryptocurrencies: the case of Bitcoin'. *Electron Markets* 30, 259–271 (2020). doi.org/10.1007/s12525-019-00392-5.
9 Roderick Kramer and Tom Tyler (eds), *Trust in Organizations: Frontiers of Theory and Research* (Sage 1996).
10 William Rees-Mogg and James Dale Davidson, *The Sovereign Individual* (Touchstone 1999).
11 Glen E. Weyl, 'Sovereign Nonsense', www.radicalxchange.org/media/blog/sovereign-nonsense.
12 The Visual Capitalist, www.visualcapitalist.com.
13 podcast.banklesshq.com/.

14 David Chaum, 'Computer Systems Established, Maintained and Trusted by Mutually Suspicious Groups', chaum.com/wp-content/uploads/2022/02/techrep.pdf.

15 David Chaum et al., 'Blind Signatures for Untraceable Payments'. In: Chaum, D., Rivest, R.L., Sherman, A.T. (eds) *Advances in Cryptology*. Springer, Boston, MA. doi.org/10.1007/978-1-4757-0602-4_18 (1983).

16 Dana Vioreanu, 'The Origins of Privacy and How it Became a Human Right', www.cyberghostvpn.com/en_US/privacyhub/the-origins-of-privacy-and-how-it-became-a-human-right/.

17 The Ethereum Whitepaper, ethereum.org/en/whitepaper.

18 cms-lawnow.com/en/ealerts/2022/06/english-high-court-treats-non-fungible-tokens-as-legal-property-in-fraud-case.

19 Digital Assets: Consultation Paper, www.lawcom.gov.uk/project/digital-assets/.

20 Phillip J. Windley, 'Sovrin: An Identity Metasystem for Self-Sovereign Identity', www.frontiersin.org/articles/10.3389/fbloc.2021.626726.

21 Vitalek Buterin et al., 'Decentralized Society: Finding Web3's Soul', papers.ssrn.com/sol3/papers.cfm?abstract_id=4105763.

22 Tracey Follows, *The Future of You: Can Your Identity Survive 21st-Century Technology?* (Elliot and Thomson, 2022).

23 Amy Whitaker, 'The artistic value of an NFT', parisplus.artbasel.com/stories/art-market-report-amy-whitaker.

24 Steve Kaczynski and Scott Duke Kominers, 'How NFTs Create Value', hbr.org/search?term=scott%20duke%20kominers.

25 Miles Jennings and Chris Dixon, Can't be Evil, a16zcrypto.com/content/article/introducing-nft-licenses.

26 Alex O'Donnell interview, thedefiant.io/real-yield-defi.

27 Eric, Hughes, 'The Cypherpunk Manifesto', nakamotoin-stitute.org/static/docs/cypherpunk-manifesto.txt.

28 George, Jacob, 'The History of the Rochdale Pioneers', ia802606.us.archive.org/35/items/historyofrochdalooholy-uoft/historyofrochdalooholyuoft.pdf).

29 Neal Stephenson, *Snow Crash* (Random House World 2001).

30 'Metaverse and Money', www.citifirst.com.hk/home/upload/citi_research/AZRC7.pdf.

31 Eze Vidra, www.vccafe.com/2022/06/30/investing-in-the-pillars-of-the-metaverse/.

32 Herman Narula, *Virtual Society: The Metaverse and the New Frontiers of Human Experience* (Currency 2022).

33 Theo Priestly and Bronwyn Williams, *The Future Starts Now: Expert Insights into the Future of Business, Technology and Society* (Bloomsbury Business 2001).

34 Edward Castronova, *Synthetic Worlds: The Business and Culture of Online Games* (University of Chicago Press 2006).

35 Molly White, web3isgoinggreat.com.

36 Moxie Marlinspike, 'Here's what's wrong with Web3', crypto-slate.com/moxie-marlinspike-heres-whats-wrong-with-web3.

37 Evegeny Morozov, the-crypto-syllabus.com/web3-a-map-in-search-of-territory/.

38 Balaji Srinivasan, 'The Network State: How To Start a New Country' (Kindle).

39 Vitalek Buterin, vitalik.ca/general/2022/07/13/network-states.html.

40 Sir Jon Cunliffe quote, www.telegraph.co.uk/business/2021/06/21/bank-england-tells-ministers-intervene-digital-currency-programming.

41 Bill Gates 'Tidal Wave' memo, www.sindark.com/genre/
    1995-The-Internet-Tidal-Wave.pdf.

42 Kathryn White, 'The Macroeconomic Impact of
    Cryptocurrency and Stablecoins', www.weforum.org/
    agenda/2022/11/the-macroeconomic-impact-of-crypto-
    currency-and-stablecoin-economics'

43 David Birch, dgwbirch.com.

44 Michel Khazzaka, 'Bitcoin: Cryptopayments Energy
    Efficiency' (April 20, 2022). Available at SSRN: ssrn.com/
    abstract=4125499 or dx.doi.org/10.2139/ssrn.4125499.

45 'Revealing the true costs of financial crime', www.refinitiv.com/
    content/dam/marketing/en_us/documents/reports/true-
    cost-of-financial-crime-global-focus.pdf.

46 'The 2022 Crypto Crime Report', go.chainalysis.com/2022-
    Crypto-Crime-Report.html.

47 Avraham Eisenberg, twitter.com/avi_eisen/status/
    1581326210763673602.

48 Pierluigi Freni, Enrico Ferro, Roberto Moncada,
    'Tokenomics and blockchain tokens: A design-oriented
    morphological framework, Blockchain: Research and
    Applications', 2022,ISSN 2096-7209, doi.org/10.1016/j.
    bcra.2022.100069. (www.sciencedirect.com/science/article/
    pii/S2096720922000094).

49 Sumit Kumar, web-assets.bcg.com/1e/a2/
    5b5f2b7e42dfad2cb3113a291222/on-chain-asset-tokeni-
    zation.pdf.

50 BCG, www.sifma.org/resources/research/fact-book/
    #:~:text=Section%201%20%E2%80%93%20Global%
    20Capital%20Markets&text=Global%20equity%20
    marke%20capitalization%20increased,of%20
    25.6%25%20Y%2FY.

Steven Boykey Sidley is an award-winning and multi-shortlisted author and playwright. He is the author of the novels *Entanglement*, *Stepping Out*, *Imperfect Solo*, *Free Association*, *Leaving Word* and the play *Shape* (co-written with his wife Kate Sidley), as well as the 2022 non-fiction release *Beyond Bitcoin: Decentralised Finance and The End of Banks* (co-written with Simon Dingle). He is currently a partner at Bridge Capital Future Advisory, in charge of their technology practice, and is an investor in a number of technology and crypto companies. Sidley was appointed to the position of Professor at the University of Johannesburg, Graduate School of Business (JBS) in 2022, to pursue research and teaching in blockchain and 4IR technologies.